S/11

PROVOCATIONS

THE WAR ON THE YOUNG

JOHN SUTHERLAND

SERIES EDITOR:

YASMIN ALIBHAI-BROWN

Biteback Publishing

First published in Great Britain in 2018 by
Biteback Publishing Ltd
Westminster Tower
3 Albert Embankment
London SE1 7SP
Copyright © John Sutherland 2018

ISBN 978-1-78590-339-7

10 9 8 7 6 5 4 3 2 1

A CIP catalogue record for this book is available from the British Library.

Set in Stempel Garamond

Printed and bound in Great Britain by
CPI Group (UK) Ltd, Croydon CR0 4YY

'Selfish old cunts fucking things up for youth?
Well there's a first!'

— IRVINE WELSH, AUTHOR OF *TRAINSPOTTING*,
TWEETING AFTER THE JUNE 2016 REFERENDUM. IT WAS
SUGGESTED THAT THE MYOPIC GREY VOTE HAD SCUPPERED
YOUTH'S FAR-SIGHTED DESIRE TO REMAIN IN EUROPE.
IRVINE WELSH IS FIFTY-EIGHT YEARS OLD. @IRVINEWELSH

'There is a war.'

— LEONARD COHEN, IN THE SONG OF THE SAME NAME

'Nobody ever talks about generational conflict.
Who wants to bring up that the old are eating
the young at the dinner table?'

— STEPHEN MARCHE, *ESQUIRE* MAGAZINE, 2012

– Saturn (AKA Cronus) Devouring his Son

BY FRANCISCO GOYA

'Bliss was it in that dawn to be alive,
But to be young was very heaven!'

– WILLIAM WORDSWORTH

But not if you're Dad's breakfast.

Contents

Preface:
An Illustrative Anecdote

T HE FOLLOWING WAS reported in *The Times*,
4 October 2017:

LIVE FRUGALLY, STUDENTS TOLD

Students who are short of money could adopt a frugal
existence, Jo Johnson told the Tory conference yesterday.

The universities minister was responding at a fringe
event to Martin Lewis founder of the website Money
Saving Expert, who said that some students could not
afford to live on their maintenance loan. These range
from £7,000 to £11,000 a year. Maintenance grants were

scrapped this year, meaning even the poorest students must take out loans to cover their living costs while at university.

Politics Home reported Mr Johnson saying: 'There may be a gap but that doesn't necessarily mean it's a gap that must be filled by parental contribution. They could work as many, many students do, they can also save. What is also so important to bear in mind is that students have many different choices about the kind of lifestyle they want at university. Some students want to live very modestly and have a frugal existence, focusing on their studies.'

Let them eat gruel. But how, however straitened their 'lifestyle', can they buy books, computers and other tools of the student trade? How, if they're whizzing around on mopeds delivering pizza all hours of the night, will they have the time or energy to study?

The *Times* report concluded, grimly, that '40 per cent of the poorest students graduate with average debt of £57,000, compared with £50,000 for all students'. These poorest students will, quite likely, get the poorest results. They do not have the head-start enjoyed by luckier peers. Poor students from universities which score towards the bottom of the performance league tables (let's not call them 'poorest') can expect poor placement after graduation. In 2015, half the graduates from London Metropolitan had found no professional work six months after leaving. Why were they encouraged to indebt themselves for life? What follows will offer an explanation.

Johnson (nicknamed, apparently, 'Johnson Minimus') is a member of a famous and high-performing clan (his brother Boris was getting bigger conference headlines in 2017).

As to 'lifestyle'. When at Oxford, judged in 2017 to be the best university in the world,[1] Jo Johnson was member of the exclusive Bullingdon Club, not known for its modesty or frugality. The livery is estimated to cost £3,500 and is only available from one Oxford tailor. It is a worthy investment. At one point in 2016, there were

---

1   Where, unlike his brother, he got a First; he's proved elsewhere to be a very able minister.

four members of the Bullingdon Club in the Cabinet. Mufti was permitted in No. 10.

Dickens should be living.

But perhaps we should make do with Johnson's fellow Tory Benjamin Disraeli's verdict: 'We are two nations.' Disraeli meant the rich and the poor, and foresaw violence if the gulf between them were not bridged. But there are another two nations in conflict at the moment: the young and the old.

Introduction

I PUBLISHED *The War on the Old* in 2017, in Bite-back's Provocations series. They're 'now' books: newscast-fast. But reflective as well as provocative. *The War on the Old* was well received, from the *Daily Mail*(s) to *The Oldie*, via *The Guardian*.

I'm aware that most of those papers' readers (and their writers) merit the self-deprecating label 'oldies'. Who, still in their freshness of youth, reads tree products nowadays? As quaint as having a Swedish wood-fired computer.

Most oldies, in my experience, feel hard done by. Embattled. However, there are typically two sides in a battle, both of whom have a *casus belli*. In this follow-up polemic I switch sides to look, with my rheumy eye, at the intergenerational conflict as it may appear to this country's and North America's brighter-eyed populations. These (the UK and the US) are where I have spent most of my life. And my career has been spent in the company of the smart young adult. They are a category of human being now under attack. I sense a rumbling tremor of something earth-shaking to come.

I lived for forty years (1949–89) of my life in fear it could end with four minutes' warning. Flash, heat, blast, radiation and it would be all over. I was employed in southern California, 'earthquake country', for twenty-five years (1983–2008) in daily expectation of the 'Big One' – the seismic event that will destroy the state and put America back fifty years. I feel, not to be apocalyptic, a somewhat similar apprehension today: a breakdown of the intergenerational civilities that make our civilisation work. Patronage on one side, deference on the other. Perhaps I should get a couple of sandwich boards and walk up and down Oxford Street or Rodeo Drive warning 'The End is Nigh!' I've written these two 'War' books instead.

In the fog of war, opponents identify themselves by

recognisable uniform and insignia. In the generational war I write about, no uniform is necessary. Count the wrinkles, look at the head of hair, listen for the slur. Who's their favourite pop star? Madonna and David Bowie means old; Elvis Presley and Barbra Streisand means really old. Me? I still have a soft spot for Bill Haley, the first rock star to die in an old folks' home, rocking around the clock no more.

In *The War on the Old*, I used Sinbad and the Old Man of the Sea as an illustration. Briefly summarised (there are many written and oral variations) this is how the main narrative line goes. Young Sinbad the Sailor, sole survivor of a shipwreck, finds himself washed up in what looks like the garden of paradise. Among its lushness, he comes across a wizened old man sitting down – unable to stand, apparently. Poor old chap. The old man feebly requests to be hoisted onto the young voyager's shoulders so he can pluck the fruit that hangs out of his palsied reach.

Good naturedly, Sinbad does as the old geezer asks. Big mistake. The old man's legs suddenly clamp in a vice-like grip round the young man's throat. Sinbad must now carry the fruit-guzzling oldster until one of them dies. Most likely it will be Sinbad, from exhaustion and inanition (the OMS is not a sharer of the good things in life).

What happens next is crucial. Sinbad cannily gets the old man (who likes a drop) falling-down drunk with fermented fruit juice and, once free of the vice around his neck, the youngster takes up a great stone and batters the oldster's brains out.

A happy ending.

There are two salient features in the fable: the first, clearly, is that the old use the young to get what they, the old, need or crave. The second, which merits more careful thought, is that the old are deuced cunning. It's called crabbed age for a good reason – they can have a nasty nip. Not just the thighs.

The old man may be taken as every old man (and many old women, in these egalitarian times), AD 2017 and the young Sinbad as youth, AD 2017.

And where are we now as a society? Just at that point, I suggest, where the legs of the old man are beginning their throttling grip round the neck of the young man.

It is not Cronus, devouring his young. That's a metaphor. It is the aged exploiting the young, for their own advantage and comfort. For the fruits, as the good things of life are allegorised in the Sinbad tale. Leave the skin and core for the young.

What is the allegory saying, in real-life terms? Think of the NHS. Young people are, on the whole, healthy. Old people (like he in the story), on the whole, are not. They are kept going expensively. By drugs, concessions, welfare payments, bed blocking and residential 'social' care. 'Kerching!' as the comedians say, rubbing thumb and forefinger together.

David Willetts – a politician who is thoughtful about the conflict between generations – estimates that the baby boomers (the current generation of retirees) get 20 per cent more out of the British health service than they paid into it. And they are living 20 per cent longer, in terms of years, largely because of that. Call them the Older Men of the Sea.

The burden of the old is getting heavier on younger shoulders by the year. When will Sinbad reach for the stone?

We lapse into sociologese to talk about 'intergenerational friction', muffling the brute fact with Latinism and euphemism. But it is cruel and simple. Either the young must be exploited, as beasts of burden, and live reduced lives, or the old must be disposed of. Sentimentalising the conflict – plunging it into Golden Pond (only the old will recall that movie) – is to ignore it. Moving as we are to a pensionless future for today's middle-aged and younger, the situation will get crueller.

Call it war. If only for brevity.

The main contention in this book is that the deteriorating life-plight of young people today is not accidental, like a sudden downfall of rain. What, precisely, is this plight? The young have been reduced to a 'precariat' – a precarious sector of society which has creature comforts no previous generation has enjoyed, but no distant-horizon life prospects. According to the Institute for Fiscal Studies, the young person, AD 2017, can expect eleven changes of job during their working life. This is an extraordinary statistic.[2] I call it, later on, a life without

---

2   I've had three in a typically unsettled profession.

ladders. Why has it been allowed to happen? Because it creates insecurity. To paraphrase Noam Chomsky, 'keep young people insecure and they're going to be under control'.[3] Control is victory.

It has either been deliberately let happen or deliberately made happen. A willed thing. Deliberate. Long-sighted policies are coming to fruition. Whose policies? And why?

Follow the advantage. Behind it, you will often find the old's self-seeking, self-rewarding strategies. The old are, by and large, the policy makers. You won't, of course, find 'screw the young' expressed as an aim in any of Britain's three main parties' manifestos. But it's there, beneath the surface. One of those parties, as I write, is led by a 61-year-old woman, declaring, between racking coughs, that she will hold tenaciously to her office until 2020. The main opposition to Theresa May is led by a 68-year-old man. The third party is led by a 74-year-old man. Ponder those ages.

---

3   In what he says is his last address to the world, 'Requiem for the American Dream'. He says 'workers' not 'young people'.

Part I

Part I

BRITONS

"WANTS

YOU"

JOIN YOUR COUNTRY'S ARMY!

GOD SAVE THE KING

Reproduced by permission of LONDON OPINION

But is It *Really* War? Or Just Hard Times for the Young – They'll Pass?

WAR – AT ITS simplest – is a socially (twice in the last century worldwide) disruptive, risk-all, event in which, typically, old or older people (mainly men) recruit and use young people (overwhelmingly male) to achieve ends the old men want.

Look at that archetypal 1914 recruiting poster.

It could apply to every great war. How old was Kitchener in 1914? Sixty-four. How old was the King whom the young were told to give their lives for? Forty-nine. Children, some as young as sixteen, were falsifying their ages to join up en masse.

Is there, however, such a thing as an intra-social war?

Guerre sans frontières. Thomas Hobbes, in *Leviathan*, argued that yes, there is – taking as central the proverbial truth that society in its natural state is a 'war of all against all'. The Hobbesian thesis can be glossed as 'competition' or 'free enterprise' but it is covert warfare. It has boiled up to the point of explosion in our day.

Standing back, one can see intergenerational strife as a perennial feature of social organisation. One side has the vitalities and beauties of youth (but little beyond that); the other side has gathered the lion's share of the country's treasure, having used the life-years they have behind them to accumulate it. And, of course, the old have the good things their wealth can buy: the fruit.

Gerontocracy:
Three Exemplary Examples

1. Jezza

On the news as I write (28 September 2017) there are a couple of headline stories that catch the eye.

One is Jeremy Corbyn's oratorical triumph at his third Labour Party conference. Jezza, as his partisans fondly call him, has risen to the top of the party where he was for decades an unregarded gadfly. His rise was fuelled, principally, by young members in extraordinary numbers, pissed off with Blairism. Blair, of course, was, after the cheers which saw him out of Parliament, a very rich old man (now sixty-four). A man of the people? No. As the folk song (sung to the tune of the communist 'Internationale') put it, the working class could kiss his arse.

Youthquake, the Corbyn revolution was called.

There was a 10 per cent electoral gain for the party in Theresa May's ill-called snap election of 2017. That gain was the result of votes cast by a new caucus of under-35s. A political Kraken had awoken.

Jeremy Corbyn is sixty-eight years old, and makes no attempt to disguise his years. His own youthquaking days are long gone – those distant days, for example, when he and his then paramour Diane Abbott rode saddle and pillion to East Germany to experience real socialism. It was the 1970s, when more were trying to escape that socialism, at the cost of being shot on the wire, than visiting the DDR.

One of the first things the Old Man of the Sea does is to direct Sinbad's legs to the other side of the paradisal island – call it the left side. Where, then, is old man Jez directing (not leading) the Labour youth whose enthusiasm has made him politically real? We may have to wait until he has successfully directed himself to No. 10 to find out. His opponents make dire predictions, thinking of Kremlin Square.

One thing is clear: Corbyn is an old man, in charge of a cohort of young storm troopers ('Momentum') wherewith to carry out his will. Why not break the mould and have a twenty-something as leader of the PLP? Think that through. The Labour Party may need its Kim Jong-un.

2. Hef

The other big story on 28 September was the death of Hugh Hefner, aged a venerable ninety-one. 'Hef' got rich, famous and powerful by making the beaver shot look ideologically progressive. Together with his advocacy of lifelong juvenile hedonism, Hefner's 'playboy philosophy' (boys and boys come out to play) endorsed Leontes's declaration in *The Winter's Tale* that all men yearn to be 'boy eternal'.

Hefner's glossy magazine *Playboy* (not 'Playman') was a trendsetter, his dusky, sex-laden clubs, with their desirable but untouchable buttock-fluffy 'Bunnies' were fashionable. Why not have an erection with your dry martini? To paraphrase Thom Gunn, Hefner turned lust into a lifestyle.[4]

A clever man, Hefner could write, unlike other multi-millionaire high-end pornographers (Bob Guccione, Larry Flynt, Paul Raymond). One might go so far as to say Hefner could think. Philosophise, as he called it.

His magazine carried the work of classy writers – Vonnegut, Nabokov, Atwood etc. They were there not because they wanted to be in a skin mag but because *Playboy* paid top dollar because it was a skin mag.

Hefner's main purpose in life, as he passed on from

---

4   According to Gunn's poem 'Elvis Presley', 'he turned revolt into a style'.

middle to old age, was self-gratification and self-glorification. The cult of him. He erected Playboy mansions, East and West, after the style of presidential White Houses.

At his peak, Hef had a plane modelled on the Supreme Commander's Air Force One – 'the Big Bunny', Hef called his airliner. Mile-high sex? As routine as lasagne or chicken for the lesser air travellers.

Yachts? A veritable fleet of them. His favourite uniform was the captain's cap and the velvet dressing gown – bespeaking quarter deck and bedroom. Power and the penis. How does that schoolyard dirty ditty go:

> Aboard the good ship Venus,
> By God you should have seen us,
> The figure head was a maid in bed
> And the main mast was a penis.

Hefner created for himself what the critic Steven Marcus calls a 'pornotopia'.[5] He surrounded himself with

5   In *The Other Victorians* (1966).

a sultanic harem. There was, one Playmate recalled, no free movement in and out of the mansion. No male or family visitors were allowed. Eunuchs (security men) were in attendance to keep Playmates in the playpen.

No Playmate could expect to grow old in the mansion. They came, they were used, they left to make way for fresher successors. Hef publicised the fact that he had fucked (why use a fuzzier word) a thousand women or more. The BBC reported this fact the day after he died as blandly as the number of goals Arsenal had scored in last night's match. A man who has a thousand women is, we were to apprehend, a 'playboy'. Women who have a thousand men are called harsher names.

For fifty years of his sexual career, Hugh Hefner was not a boy. He was a goat, goatier the older he got. His ever-changing cohort of bed-warming Playmates had two things in common. They were beautiful, laid out, like items on a menu, in his magazine, and therefore desired by other, unluckier men – let lesser guys masturbate over the glossy centrefold. It certified Hef's conquest over other males.

Secondly, his Playmates were, even in his early years

as master of the mansion and vessel, younger than he. At the end, grotesquely so. He represented the penile domination of the old over the young. Grizzled and thin-haired, he was – despite every skill of the cosmetician – ugly. But he was Hef the Conqueror.

Hef would run up to seven 'girlfriends' simultaneously. It was important he be thought prepotent. Hef occasionally married – but only his first marriage was to a woman around his own age.

His last solemnised union was to a former Playmate of the Month, in 2012. She would be Mrs Crystal Hefner for only four years. At the time of the wedding, he was eighty-six; she was twenty-six. An ironclad prenup stopped widow Crystal inheriting much in the not unlikely event that her husband predeceased her. But who knew, apart from Viagra and Pepsi (his preferred libation), what elixirs of life Hef was quaffing?

The glamour pasted, like condom skin, onto the Playboy industry was a publicity illusion, as a series of indignant former Playmates reported in their tell-all memoirs. As the feminist Gloria Steinem recorded, after some field work, being an untouched 'Bunny' in a Playboy club was ugly. In their 'den', supervised by a den mother, Bunnies desperately stuffed their bras with anything from plastic bags to tampons to ensure pert uplift.

Then, in the club area, there was the sexual humiliation of simpering under the leering male gaze, the plastic bag scraping your breast as you leaned forward with the expensive drink. Most humiliating, the bunny job was grossly underpaid, Steinem discovered.

Linda 'Lovelace' (Linda Boreman), among others, recorded the cold brutality of the Playboy mansion orgy. Hefner's main interest in her, she recalled in her book *Ordeal*, was bestial. Literally. Enforced by her pimp, Chuck Traynor, she had made a film of herself copulating with a dog. It was, apparently, a sexual theme of interest to Hefner. A dog lover.

The proposition, supported by some, that the 'Playboy Philosopher' was a friend to feminism rings false. Another Playmate, Holly Madison, described in her book *Down the Rabbit Hole* the mansion joy of sex. Hef would summon his harem, enticingly unclad, gather them in a semi-circle and put 'graphic porn' on the bedroom TV. He would then puff some marijuana and 'tend to his own business', as Madison put it. His entourage would writhe erotically before the chosen was selected. To chants of 'go Daddy go!' the couple would adjourn for more business.

'It's like being with Grandad,' said another twenty-something Playmate, Carla Howe. More like being with Charlie Manson, some would say.

What, then, did the Playboy industry and Hef's ritualisation of the sexual act signify? The power of an old man over the young.[6]

3. *The Donald*

During his electoral campaign in 2016, one of the things that was confidently expected to hole Donald Trump below the water line was his piratically recorded recommendation of 'pussy grabbing'. It was the quickest and surest way to sexual conquest, he averred.

---

6   In the interval between writing and publication, the Weinstein scandal has exploded. It's in the air at the moment, swirlingly. But one thing is clear: the complainants (against Weinstein and others) are mainly younger – by far – or were younger at the time of the alleged offences.

Trump was seventy years old when he confided this wisdom. A stage of life when, as commonly thought, the heyday in the blood is tame, and male hair has gone grey or just gone – not gold, like Trump's mane, as unconvincing as a cranial codpiece.[7]

More telling (but similarly of no ultimate consequence to his electability) was a radio conversation Trump had had in 2002 with shock-jock Howard Stern. Trump was then in his mid-fifties. Stern did not, as with other of his guests, inquire about the girth and length of Trump's penis. At least, not on air.

Nonetheless, in his 2016 election appearances more than once Trump went out of his way to remind voters of his bigness. Trump recalled to Stern that he had dated 21-year-olds but it was 'embarrassing [because] they would be studying algebra'. Algebra grabbing was not something that attracted him. He concluded that thirty was the 'perfect age' for a woman. Perfect for the man twice her age, that is.

---

7   Americans do not like bald Presidents, any more than they like female or Jewish Presidents. Invariably, the taller candidate wins.

But the aperture was narrow. Thirty-five, Trump confided (on air) to Stern, was 'check-out time'.

The imagery evokes a male fantasy supermarket; one whose shelves contain row upon row of women, all with sell-by dates pasted on their bodies. Hillary Clinton, a rising seventy, was thirty-five years past hers. She'd be in the waste bins behind the store, for the dumpster divers to take or leave. It's a vile image, but one which Clinton's opponent subtly, and knowingly, propagated. The easiest mistake to make about Trump is that he's a fool.

Trump, in office, is now seventy-one. Twice his 'perfect' woman's age. His consort at public events is Ivanka, his daughter by his first marriage. Ivanka is only just past her prime at thirty-six years old.

Trump earlier agreed with Howard Stern that she was, then twenty years old: 'a great piece of ass'. This is how the men's lubricious exchange went:

> Trump: 'My daughter is beautiful.'
>
> Stern: 'By the way, your daughter…'
>
> Trump: 'She's beautiful.'

Stern: 'Can I say this? A piece of ass.'
Trump: 'Yeah.'

Beauty = a great piece of ass. 'Yeah.'

Trump has had a number of on-air conversations with Stern. Typically they revolved around sex and age difference. In 2006 (Trump now fifty-seven, Stern, a couple of years younger), the following was broadcast to the listening millions:

Stern: 'Do you think you could now be banging 24-year-olds?'
Trump: 'Oh, absolutely.'
Stern: 'Would you do it?'
Trump: 'I'd have no problem.'
Stern: 'Do you have an age limit?'
Trump: 'No, no, I have no age – I mean, I have an age limit. I don't want to be like Congressman Foley, with, you know, twelve-year-olds.'

American parents of pre-teens can sleep secure. Their daughters are at no risk from presidential *droit du seigneur*. Once those young things are twenty, and great pieces of ass, may be the time to worry.

The three foregoing examples might be thought to be (thank God) atypical. But they are parabolic – that is to say, like parables they express something illustrative about the current power relation between society's two opposed groups: the old and the young.

Moving to society as a whole, the executive power, the right to regulate and institute change, is with old males and the occasional old female. Look at the front benches in the House of Commons. And the House of Commons is merely the anteroom to that (Very) Old Folks Home – 'the other place', the House of Lords (I read in my paper today that they are seriously considering retiring the ermined struldbrugs over eighty. No way).

Contemplate the group pictures of the Bilderberg Club. Or the American Senate – aptly named for its seniors. Or the age and gender composition of the British and American Supreme Courts. These bodies make, pass and amend laws for all. The well-being, or ill-being, of the young is in wrinkled hands.

This Is the Way the World Ends?

Consider next the age difference between Kim Jong-un ('Little Rocket Man', as Trump calls him, employing a favourite penis-size jest) and Donald Trump ('degenerate dotard', as Kim calls Trump).

These are paramount leaders whose intergenerational bickering, as I write, may reduce the planet to a nuclear smouldering ashcan at any moment.

Kim and Trump are currently the most dangerous men in the world. At the UN, a body with world peace at its mission, Trump threatened to nuke North Korea into radioactive rubble. Kim promised in return fire and brimstone for America. The two leaders have moved the Doomsday Clock forward towards apocalyptic midnight. It's currently at its nearest ever, at three minutes to twelve. Night night, world.

Kim Jong-un is dangerous not because like China

or Russia he has a formidable army, but because he has bought and developed the state-of-the-art toys of all-out war. They are 'equalisers', as gangsters used to call their shooters. MIRV-armed ICBMs with global range equalise a tinpot dictatorship and the world's sole superpower.

Now, or within a year or so, Kim Jong-un will be able, by pre-emptive strike, to kill millions of South Koreans in Seoul with a massive artillery barrage, wipe out Japan with intermediate-range weapons and incinerate Los Angeles. For starters. Kim ignores pressure to pull in his horns from his principal ally – China, whose paramount leader, Xi Jinping, aged sixty-five, is just another paramount dotard in his book.

How old is Kim? (I write in 2017). Thirty-three. He became supreme leader, with plenipotentiary power to do what he liked with his toy box of nuclear weaponry, aged twenty-seven. And play with his nuclear toy he did – it was the best Xbox in history.

The Word of Freud

As regards intergenerational warfare, Freudians point

knowingly to the toddler Oedipus's lusting for the mother who is the vengeful father's exclusive sexual property. Young Oedipus is kept in line by the fear (in his little mind) of castration. It has been suggested this might be something specifically Viennese, the domestic hothouse where Freud came up with his most famous theory. Most psychoanalysts grant it universality.

A 'complex', as Freud called these psychic conflicts, emerges. The resolution of the complex, as the loyal psychoanalysts argue, civilises the wannabe mother-raping, father-killing infant. (Freud did not get girls into the picture, although an effort was made by his disciple, Carl Jung, with the Electra complex.) Civilisation as Freudian is based on suppression, sublimation and the denial of violent infantile desire. The end result was universal *Unbehagen* (discontent, anxiety), as Freud called it. Society's great building block. But what if that system breaks down and those uncivilised juvenile desires are loosed?

Power over the lives of the young is the main weapon the old have. They have in their hands the levers of society's great machinery. It's not quite a gelding knife, but it serves. There are no school-leaver age MPs with the power to pass laws (e.g. to levy £9,250 per year for their higher education) in Western democracies. North Korea under young post-graduate age Kim is something else.

Their elders have another, biological, advantage over the young. Every old person was young once and, from experience, knows the weak points of youth. No young person has been old, and they complacently underestimate their wily foe. A good young 'un will always beat a good old 'un, they say, repeating the boxers' maxim. Not always: either in the ring or in life.

Kim Jong-un is wrong if he thinks Donald Trump really is a drooling 'dotard'. Granted he is well into the vale of years, the 45th President did not get to be the most powerful man in the world by being stupid. It's only in fiction, like Jerzy Kosiński's *Being There*, that an idiot can assume supreme power in the USA. Trump is vulgar and boorish. He may also be narcissistic, borderline psychotic and/or cognitively impaired by age (I do not, incidentally, assert any of these things. Others do). But he's canny. Too canny, one hopes, to connive in the wiping out of seven billion people.

Part II

The Big Picture

SINCE THE GREAT Depression there has been, while Wall Street and London's 'City' boomed, and national net worth in the US and the UK boomed with it, a huge depression of the young person's life prospects. All the spring is gone from the springboard which traditionally propelled the youthful on their upward way in life to occupy, in the fullness of time, the still-warm seats of the departed old.

On 29 September 2017, a mass survey of 18–30-year-olds by the Young Women's Trust (nice name) came up with a depressing set of results. The BBC that day reported them under the grim banner 'I worry about money most of the time'. There was indeed cause for worry in the cascade of statistics:

- A third of young people felt more anxious than at the same time the previous year.
- 25 per cent of young women and 21 per cent of young men said their financial situation was worse.
- 45 per cent of young women were worried about their mental health, as were 38 per cent of young men.
- A third of young women reported gender discrimination at work or while looking for work.

One must, again, assume that something consciously created this situation; that this outcome has been made to happen. It's a *regime*, with a purpose driving it, not an unhappy set of accidental events. Is it paranoia to think so? Paranoia is sometimes right.

Money – a slice of the pie – is, as the BBC headline states, the main factor in the new imbalance between generations. Like global warming, this is not a change beyond social control; both are long-term bequests from the old to the young, and their younger offspring – welcome to a planet we've used up.

It was, briefly to pursue this theme, old males who allowed global overpopulation and global debt (currently $20 trillion or so in the US) and declined to rectify either. A fine global mess they (we, if I'm honest) have left the young, for generations hence. There's more. Two thirds of the arable land on earth, *The Guardian* cheerfully informs its readers, has been over-farmed into unproductive dust and dirt. There are, the paper's resident Jeremiad, George Monbiot, reminds its readers, only sixty harvests left.[8] Anyone under thirty today has a good chance of seeing that happen. Enjoy your cornflakes while you still have them.

George Orwell made the point that if you want to render a population docile, indebt them. Financial anxiety works better than Room 101. A heavy mortgage douses the fire in every dissident's belly.[9]

Orwell was thinking, in 1938, of middle-aged, lower-middle-class, mid-century wage slaves. But in 2017, as the Young Women's Trust tells us:

- 24 per cent of young people are in debt all the time.

---

8   https://www.theguardian.com/commentisfree/2017/oct/20/insectageddon-farming-catastrophe-climate-breakdown-insect-populations

9   In the novel *Coming up for Air* (1939).

- 48 per cent of young people are running out of cash each month.
- Using overdrafts to make ends meet was a fact of life for one in five of those surveyed, similar numbers borrowed from family, while almost as many ran up their credit cards.
- One in ten had used a payday loan company, rising to one in four among young parents.
- Just over one in ten said they skipped meals when they ran out of cash, though about 14 per cent said they could work extra hours if they were short.[10]

Follow the money. In 1984, the average net worth of US citizens aged sixty-five and over was $120,457 (including assets like cars, house, savings and pension). The corresponding net worth of those aged thirty-five and younger was $11,521. A ratio, roughly, of one to ten. Given the many earning years the young have ahead of them, and the credit those years could buy, it was not an Everest. Enough pie to be getting on with.

---

10 https://www.youngwomenstrust.org/what_we_do/media_centre/press_releases/669_young_women_s_trust_survey_reveals_youth_debt_epidemic

In 2009, the respective figures were $170,494 at the top, $3,662 at the bottom. The bottom had suddenly got mine-shaft deeper. The ratio was now forty-seven to one. A similar slippage can be plausibly assumed over the same period in the UK, slightly mitigated by welfare statism.[11]

Stephen Marche, in the 2012 article from which the above gloomy figures are taken, deduced:

> This bleeding up of the national wealth is no accounting glitch, no anomalous negative bounce from the recent unemployment and mortgage crises, but rather the predictable outcome of thirty years of economic and social policy that has been rigged to serve the comfort and largesse of the old at the expense of the young.

Noam Chomsky, in a sermon no one listened to, drew the same conclusions.[12] We live, he outlined – with the

---

11 http://www.esquire.com/news-politics/a13226/young-people-in-the-recession-0412/

12 *Requiem for the American Dream.*

precision of one of the great minds of our time – in a world which is, for the young, a chanceless tyranny.

The one moment Chomsky saw a hopeful, but temporary, breakthrough was in the 1960s, when youth was (as their elders and betters believed) anarchically (or, as Chomsky saw it, democratically) out of (their) control. And dedicated, even worse, to war on the old: 'We'll hang the last gerontocrat with the guts of the last bureaucrat' ran a chilling slogan in the 'occupied' Edinburgh University in 1968. I was twenty-eight at the time and, as a junior staff member, had mixed feelings.

What was it de Gaulle said that same year, when he stamped on the *événements* – the French youth rebellion? *'La réforme, oui; la chie-en-lit, non.'*

No more 'shitting in the bed'. It's what incontinent infants do. More toilet training, that's what the young need. Toilet training till they're old enough to know better (say, forty). The old have a heavy fist, when required. De Gaulle was seventy-seven in 1968; youth's leader in the Paris streets, Daniel Cohn-Bendit ('Danny the Red') was twenty-three. Danny lost.

The American Vietnam street backlash among youth

of the late '60s was, Chomsky tells us, momentarily powerful. It was a glimpse of what could be. The young resolved not to be sacrificed in a war which was pointless. The old guys in the White House and Pentagon saw a point.

Conscription, the militarisation of the young to fight the wars embarked on by the old (their own lives unthreatened), was ended in the US after the Vietnam defeat – defeat both in the Indo-Chinese jungles and in the streets of DC.

Somewhere, behind doors, it was resolved that never again would that 1960s mistake of loosing the turbulent energies of the young be made in the US. Above all, training them in the use of guns and military tactics was a no-no.

A few concessions were made: the voting age was progressively dropped, giving the impression of new power. Students were allowed a say in the set-up of their university syllabuses. Pressed to the wall, governments can always come up with a hailstorm of tokens. Non-disruptive feminism was tolerated. More women were recruited into higher education, politics and previously closed professions. The disciplines of courtship – 'The Scent of a Woman', as the movie put it – tranquillised young men.

As Lampedusa prescribed in *The Leopard*, things needed to change to stay the same. Which, by and large, they did. But behind the scenes, slowly and furtively, long-term measures were taken against the young who had so impertinently shat the social bed. It was autonomic (like breathing when you're asleep) – the system probably did not know it was doing it. But it was done.

Shooting the 'bums' (as Nixon called the young), Potemkin Battleship-style, clearly would not work. Kent State University, where the National Guard shot down demonstrating (not rioting) students, proved that. Principal among the measures, and much more successful, was what Chomsky calls 'financialisation' – grab them by the wallets, and their hearts and minds will follow. Slap a price tag on everything. Including the price tag. Outsource, atomise, fragment. Above all, charge top dollar at every step. Justify it as efficiency – when, subversively, the intention is to disorganise. Turn movements into headless rabbles which can be more easily dealt with.

Students had traditionally been the radical spearhead, where new, disruptive ideas are generated and dangerous solidarity formed – particularly in the great metropolitan universities. Make them pay through the nose for their education – convert them into anxious customers. Consumerise everything. Retail the ivory tower. Without any fixed price, but one which always slides up.

The tactic was hugely successful as a youth tranquilliser. And remunerative for everyone but the 2.5 million UK students and 16 million US students themselves.

The joke is, it need not even be a real debt – the mere threat will do the trick. Students 'know' that many if not most of them will graduate with a £50–57k career debt, repayable after the threshold £25k p.a. is passed. Month by month, 9 per cent of the surplus will be extracted from pay packets over thirty years.

But the model by which the Student Loan Company (more of which later) conducts its usurious business predicts that 77 per cent of graduates will never pay the full amount, or anything like it.

Why, then, dangle the fearsome fifty grand plus in front of students? Because even the idea of it takes the fight out of the young person. And the notional amount creates years'-long insecurity. A mortgage broker will be reticent, for example, if two young people apply with £114,000 of joint debt outstanding. It's an albatross round the young person's neck.

Student fees, let's be blunt, are a con. Analysis by the IFS (a constant wasp in the government's jam jar) revealed, on 8 October 2017 that, as the *Sunday Times* reported:

> The cost to taxpayers of getting a student through university is now greater than before fees were tripled to £9,250 a year, research has revealed … the taxpayer contribution towards tuition fees and living costs will be greater than if the pre-2012 system [£3,000 p.a.] was still in place.

Ho-hum. Then why are they doing it? To keep the (potential) enemy down.

Cassandra Willetts

'Although it is not true that all conservatives are stupid people, it is true that most stupid people are conservative.' So said John Stuart Mill. Lord David Willetts – 'Two Brains Willetts', in newspaper disrespectful shorthand – is the black swan exception to Mill's sneer.

In 2006, Willetts outlined, with limpid clarity, his contrarian position as an anti-conservative conservative. He called the book in which he stated it *Modern Conservatism*. The party he addressed did not find itself inclined to modernise.

For a man of his political intellect, Willetts has never achieved the senior Cabinet power his brain(s) deserves. The one position he occupied for a couple of years was abolished when he left it. His being passed over is not because of that one cerebral cortex too many – although, of course, his party instinctively distrusts members who are, as was said of the similarly unappreciated Iain Macleod, 'too clever by half'. That half damned his prospects of Downing Street.

Nor has Willetts ever learned to shut up about certain doctrines a politician may safely believe in the secrecy of his/her mind but which are political death to utter aloud. Willetts said the unsayable by venturing that the affirmative action which had advanced women in the nation's workforce was an impediment rather than a liberation.

The most likely reason for Willetts's being neglected is that he utters other truths which his party, and their voters, would rather not hear. The most pungent of those truths were expressed in his 2010 treatise: *The Pinch: How the Baby Boomers Took Their Children's Future – and Why They Should Give it Back*. The long title says it all. It also indicates the conceptual flaw in the book. It wasn't the 'baby boomers' (that enlarged number of postwar WWII births, now 65ish) who 'took' their children's future, rendering the young a 'squeezed generation'. The baby boomers gratefully received it as a gift (bribe) from the politicians, post-2008.

The figures Willetts bandies about in his book carry weight. The baby boomers owned, in 2010, more than half the country's £6.7 trillion national wealth. They represented a quarter of the population. And the BBs gobbled up the treasure which had fallen in their laps; they did not pass it on to their young in what John Major once called the 'golden stream' (an image with uncomfortable evocations of pleasures offered for sale in the capital's telephone kiosks).

The BBs, Willetts calculated, had received a fifth more from the welfare state's open hand than they had contributed. It was pillage. As with PFI projects (let the future find the money for what we're enjoying), the crushing debt of national regeneration was passed on, with a host of middlemen taking a cut and adding to the eventual cost to the young.

Willetts's book and its damning statistics were no music to Conservative ears. They did not wish to know. If they knew it, they would have to do something about it. On his part, David Willetts was cast as the Cassandra of the party, the outsider, yelling truths no one wanted to hear.

The truths kept coming. On 29 September, in *The Guardian* (an uncongenial organ for most Conservatives), as members were pinning on their rosettes for the 2017 Tory Party conference, Willetts warned: 'The Conservative party risks permanently losing the support of younger voters unless Theresa May urgently tackles the challenges faced by the squeezed generation.'

Based on evidence gathered by the think tank the Resolution Foundation, which he chairs, Willetts went on to say: 'We are getting more and more disconnected.' The 'we' rings a trifle hollow. He was by this point at the same distance from the core of the party as Uranus is from the sun.

The party had hitherto turned a blind eye, muttering to themselves, 'Get stuffed, Two Brains.' Thinking like Willetts's should bloody well stay in its think tank. There was, however, on the same day as his *Guardian* article, the release of a poll by another source, the Social Market Foundation, which revealed that:

> More than twice as many voters under the age of 45 think Jeremy Corbyn's Labour party is now 'on their side' …
> The survey shows it is not just voters in their teens and 20s but also those in their 30s and young middle age who now believe that the Tories do not speak for them.

Suddenly, the penny dropped. My God, our man is telling the truth. Young electors hate us. By way of their prelude to the 2017 conference, the PM's office rushed out what was hailed on its front page by the *Telegraph*, on 1 October, a 'revolution', and by the *Mail on Sunday* as an 'audacious' move. The young, it was now clear, even to the backwoodsmen of the party, had to be brought back to the fold.

'We are listening,' said Theresa May, who had hitherto been rather hard of hearing young voices. And No. 10 had, as it thought, the answer that would bring back those children the trickster Pied Piper Corbyn had lured away.

Looked at carefully, the inducement they came up with was something less than revolutionary or audacious. Fees were to be 'frozen' from the following year onwards at £9.25k (for how long wasn't said). The threshold salary, after which repayment on the former student loan is extorted, was to be raised from £21k to £25k. These picayune adjustments were estimated to cost £2.3 billion, which gives some idea of the huge amount in toto the student loan book is worth. That was not threatened.

Big deal. What did it amount to? 'We'll bankrupt you more slowly, kids.' Willetts was right. His party was totally disconnected. Corbyn had, the week before, fired his young supporters with grand projects and a promise to 'drain the swamp'. The Westminster swamp being Blair, Blairism and all the other time-servers. The 'expenses' scandal of 2009 had tainted the existing old-school Members of Parliament – whatever their party affiliation. They stank in the nostrils of Corbynistas. They must go. Ignominiously. The deselection purge was set in process. Tumbrils were rolling.

Corbyn had not, like many in the Labour Party (and even more outrageously in the Conservative Party) dipped his snout in the parliamentary expenses trough. He had been, in fact, the lowest claimer in the House. No duck house for Jez. His total expense claim was £8.75 for an ink cartridge.

By the by, Corbyn had promised to abolish tuition fees entirely, and to wipe out the contractual debt of those currently paying them. Pie in the sky, his opponents snorted. The Venezuelan strategy. It proved the man was a fool. But it was indicative of his belief that from the start fees had been wrong. The young could buy into that. And they did.

The Squeeze

Financialisation works. But it had its ups and downs. The most precipitous down happened in 2008. The Great Recession, following the worldwide banking collapse, was narrowly averted but had to be paid for. The emergency funds that governments, led by Gordon Brown's, had shovelled, by the tens of billions, to the banking sector had to be made good from somewhere. Which particular 'where', though?

The banks, run at the top by obscenely remunerated old men (who blithely awarded themselves annual bonuses hundreds of times the average national wage), weren't going to pay – even though they had been directly responsible for the crash, with their subprime-loan recklessness. Old Mother Riley could have told them lending to clients who couldn't pay you back was money down the drain. But it was other people's money – and there was a quick buck to be made before someone (not them) had to carry the can.

Older citizens, especially paid-up householders in stable marital relationships (like me, to lay my cards on the table) largely dodged the 2008 bullet. Their assets (principally domestic property and privileged pensions which no longer existed for their juniors in the same jobs as them) were ring-fenced. The grotesque appreciation of the value of their houses (50 per cent or more for prime properties in the years from 2008 to 2017) meant, as the second decade rolled on, that they could dig into an even bigger slice of the pie than the three trillion Willetts had calculated in 2010. And it was tax-free if you cashed in your housing chips on a primary dwelling, or drew down equity from your bricks and mortar (sod the kids). It represented one of the biggest clandestine bribes in British history.

The old were, it was thought, pampered with a state pension geared to rise more than inflation; travel concessions; benefits; and a £200 annual Christmas present, courtesy of Gordon Brown. Too much feather in the nest, you might think (unless it was your nest). But the grey vote concentrated its formidable power on bird-in-the-hand issues. They did not have enough time left to play a long game. The proposal to extract the costs of end-of-life social care from the posthumous sale of beneficiaries' homes (a 'dementia tax', as it was called) almost cost the Tories the 2017 snap election. The old were untouchable. Every politician, particularly those in marginals, knew that.

Who, then, was landed with the bill? The young – so innocent most of them wouldn't even feel the pain. The costs, more visible by the year, would hang over them, Damoclean sword-style, for the rest of their lives.[13]

The property boom, which had enriched lucky house-holders, was a function of scandalous scarcity. Houses had not been built in sufficient quantity for decades – a saving for the Exchequer. And who lost out? Those for whom the houses were most urgently necessary: the young. Their prospects? 'Houseless poverty'.[14]

Consider some other statistics. In the UK, young peo-ple (22–29 years) in permanent work (not all are) draw an average gross annual income of £20,900, according to the latest figures (2015) from the Office for National Sta-tistics. In most cases, these thousands meant one income

---

13 See http://www.huffingtonpost.co.uk/entry/young-people-pay-statistics-2015-revealed_uk_573f113de4b0e71ef36d1c5e
14 King Lear, outside the hovel on the heath, 'In, boy. Go first. You houseless poverty.'

to get by on, not the older married couple's joint income (which could amount to a household £50k plus).

Fish up another set of figures. In 2017, the average price of a house across England was £240,325.

In London, where the most attractive jobs for the young are to be found, the figure is £481,556 for your own roof over your head.

The young Dick Whittingtons used to come to London, cat and pack on shoulder, because, legend had it, the streets were paved with gold. Now it is the houses which are gold plated. How, on the income levels quoted above, will the average young person ever raise the cash to buy a property to reside in? Property is not just shelter: homes are society's workshops. These years (22–29) are when children should be brought into the world and raised through their most formative years by young-adult parents.

The cost of rearing pre-school children has soared. It too has been royally financialised. Crèche means cash. The typical cost of a full-time day nursery place is, country-wide, about £210 a week for a child under two. In metropolitan areas, London notably, the average cost rises to £280 p.w.

There is no tax relief. You need an after-tax £12–15k annual disposable cash (add another thousand for the nursery/kindergarten/school run). And if you have more than one child? Tough. In short, you need the whole of an average salary – £20k(ish) – to pay child-minders so you can go out and earn that salary. Catch-22.

Forgive some anecdotalism. When I was a young parent, in the mid-1970s, 75p a weekday (the end-of-day Smartie for the kid came free) was the cost at Auntie Brenda's, at the local Herne Hill Methodist Church. An estimable house of worship, but one whose floor never felt my knees. Auntie Brenda and her Wendy House I did revere. This will sound like middle-class dinner-table complacency. But bear with me. It makes a point.

Property prices, in my young day, were affordable for the likes of 27-year-old John Sutherland. Planning marriage (to a wife doing postgraduate research, earning nothing, but paying nothing in fees), I 'acquired' (the Halifax Building Society being the actual owner for twenty-five years) the finest house I shall ever live in. A New Town, piano nobile flat in Edinburgh's Pitt Street. It cost me £2.1k in 1967. Credit-card small change nowadays. My salary, as an assistant lecturer at Edinburgh University, was, then, £1.2k p.a.

Do the maths. Average salary around £20k, in London the average house price edging half a million. Starting-level salaries nowadays in my profession are £34k and pennies (after the seven years' apprenticeship represented by a debt-incurring doctoral degree and underpaid adjunct teaching). Why was this allowed to happen? Unleash your paranoia to find the answer.

One of the arguments trotted out to justify tuition fees was that a degree brings enhanced lifetime earnings. On the *Today* programme, the Minister for Education, Jo Johnson (the other, cleverer, one) waxed rosily on the point:

> Universities continue to deliver extraordinary returns for people who go.
>
> On average, if you're a woman you're likely to have higher lifetime earnings than women who don't go to the tune of about £250,000; £170,000 if you're a man.[15]

---

15 BBC *Today* programme, 17 August 2017.

The figures, which were subsequently trotted out all around, originated in the Department for Business, Innovation and Skills in 2013.

It sounds like you've hit the jackpot.

But a BBC 'reality check', a couple of days later, found the situation more complex – and, for a bulk of graduates, not at all advantageous. The Institute for Fiscal Studies had found out, in 2016, that at twenty-three institutions for men and nine for women, the median graduate was earning less after ten years than the median non-graduate. Those foolish enough to take degrees in the creative arts 'earned no more on average than non-graduates'. But doubtless they could write poems about the inequity.

The statistics on this subject (is a degree worth £50k?) are a mare's nest – unlike the precision with which student debt is quantified to the last farthing, increased by 6.1 per cent APR (currently), and scalpelled from the pay packet before the recipient even sees it.

Chalk and Cheese

More importantly, what kind of graduate are we talking

about? They're as different in breed as dogs. The muzziness of Johnson's statistic (good minister though I believe he is) and the statistical fallacy in 'averaging' meant the future brain surgeon was on a par with the third-class graduate in sports management. Both, of course, were paying the level field £9.25k p.a.

The Times published a survey on 25 September 2017 analysing what the salaries after six months were, in various professions, for graduates who had taken different courses (there were about 110 in all). It was both illuminating and dispiriting.

The front page has a strap line along the top, with the picture of three happy, mortar-boarded youngsters (one of colour, one male and one female blonde): 'The courses that will land you a job'.

Inside is an article by the paper's education editor, entitled 'Dentists make £31,000 six months after degree'. A cool ten grand, one may note, over the young person's average salary. Vets make almost the same. Have no fear for Fido's health.

I have a personal interest in 'my' subject, English. The results are, alas, not uplifting. It comes in at no. 55

in the 110-strong list, with a measly starting salary of
£19k. As the article summarises:

> Arts graduates are notorious for being badly paid and
> this is borne out in the guide's league tables. Several arts
> subjects, including drama, dance, art and design, and
> music, account for seven of the bottom ten courses for
> earnings. Dance, drama, and cinematic graduates had the
> lowest median starting salary at £12,000.

It was the tiny sums of virtually all initial earning levels, even those of the future brain surgeon, that caught
the eye. Was it worth £50k (plus interest – and £57k
if you entered university 'poor') to qualify with these
pittances?

You don't need to talk to your pals doing economics (starting salary no. 5, £27k) to work that one out.

The Real World: AD 2017

A newspaper cynic reckoned that with things as they
are it would take forty years of saving, after debts and

day-to-day living costs, for the average young person, whether higher educated or not, to scrape up the necessary 10 per cent deposit for a mortgage. By which time the schmuck would be too short of earning years. Catch-22 again.

And all the time, for graduates (close to three quarters of a million spilling out per year), student-fee and bank-loan debt was lurking like a beast in the jungle, ready to pounce, if ever things went right for you. 'Right' being a modest £25k a year plus.

Pension(less)

The reduction or repeal of workplace pensions the young could expect decades in their future, together with the deferment of the receipt of state pensions to ever greater age (the 'older-age pension', as a wit called it) represented another slice of benefit which was deviated, in its hundreds of billions, into the wider economy – with a secondary trickle into the Exchequer via tax and other suctions.

The robbery of young people of the mid-life and

late-life benefits their elders enjoyed depends on the biological short-sightedness of the victims. The future? It will never happen. But it will. And it will be horrible.

In the *Sunday Times* in August 2017, Louise Cooper published an article entitled 'Millennials, Your Retirement is Dead in the Water'. It went on, in direct address to the unlistening young, quoting another deadly IFS bulletin:

> '[Today's young] are the first postwar cohort not to at least start working-age life with higher incomes than their predecessors had at the same age. The Great Recession hit the pay and employment of young adults the hardest … So far the early 1980s cohort have accumulated significantly less wealth than their predecessors had by the same age.'
>
> Furthermore, the nature of work has changed. The job for life has gone; about 15 per cent of the workforce is now self-employed, and temporary employment is not conducive to saving.

The average young person today, the IFS predicted, would have 'eleven different jobs' in a lifetime, without the continuities a good private pension requires. To cap it all, millennials en masse are predicted to live to ninety years old, even a hundred. It will, for a certainty, be a cursed longevity. And why not? Losers lose. And they have lost the post-'60s fight.

Youthful insouciance has made robbing the pension pot an easier game change for old lawmakers to impose. It came up, as I recall, in none of the party conferences in 2017. One aim, clearly, is to free employers from co-investment responsibility. Good for the economy; bad for the future pensioner.

I remember, in 1964, receiving my first pension contract to sign. I was a devil-may-care 25-year-old. The document, which I didn't read (even though my research, at that time, focused on literary contracts) had a terminal date which did catch my eye – 2004. I roared with laughter. We'll all be living on Mars by then, I said to a fellow signatory.

Who, below the age of thirty, nowadays, could tell you the difference between a defined benefit scheme and a defined contribution scheme? An annuity or a draw-down? Or would care? Until, that is, their sixties.

By the time I was sixty, I was beginning to work out how USS (University Superannuation Scheme) pensions were calculated – your highest salary divided by forty, then multiplied by the number of years served, a great chunk of it paid over, untaxed, on retirement, in case you still owed on your house. Imaginative and generous.

Unfortunately, I, and many like me, have ruined the system I benefited from by being all too superannu-ated. The USS is now the most indebted public pension provider in the country. It's in (as I write) a £17.5 billion debt hole. What that means is, *faute de mieux*, the youngest, still serving, academics must pay, over their careers, a bigger amount into their pensions – based on 'mean average income', not final income, with the prospect of a hurtfully smaller pot of gold for them at the end of it all.

I don't regard myself as a warmonger, but I feel guilt.

That signature, on that document, in 1964, has impov-erished the unknown retiree in forty years' time. As with other of the oppressions the old have imposed on today's young, it didn't have to turn out this way. Why then did it happen? *Cherchez le vieux*.

Austerity

'Austerity' was a necessary belt-tightening after WWII. The nation could go along with it. Austerity, in unprecedentedly prosperous peacetime, is an economic climate created deliberately by governments (whose members never suffer from what they are imposing on others). In the second decade of the twenty-first century, austerity's *force majeure* ('can't be afforded') was a third way of squeezing money from the young, by not giving them the start-up cash in pocket a decent working life needed.

Dick Whittington, the future mayor (as the bells of London told him), didn't have a job when he tramped into Highgate. Ask not for whom the bells toll nowadays. Jobseekers' allowance currently runs in the UK, 'for the eligible', sixteen to twenty-four years old, at £57.90 per week; if you're twenty-five years or over, it's £73.10. It constitutes bread-and-water rations – conceived, apparently, on the Jeremy Bentham principle (workhouse gruel and oakum picking) that pain is a stimulus which induces the able-bodied young to take the first job offered. Even if, like young Oliver Twist, it's chimney cleaning.

It was cruel, but it worked. Complacently, month after month, at PMQs, the Prime Minister would serenely announce that the employment figures were exceeding historic record levels. Britain was working. Tory cheers raised the rafters of the House. But that expanding workforce, particularly the young workers, was, to a debilitating extent, deskilled, demoralised, casualised, manualised, menialised and scraping by on minimum or little better wage rates. Other statistics indicated that the UK, in terms of productivity (and, on the side, job satisfaction) was falling behind Europe. By 2017 the UK was, shamefully, the lowest-performing economy in the G7. The country was rolling back the 200-year industrial and digital revolutions – and calling it full employment. I suspect the slaves in ancient Greece were fully employed.

Full employment 2017-style had another aspect to it: the grossly overqualified worker. At the end of July, the Institute for Public Policy Research reported: 'There are an estimated five million workers with degrees, apprenticeships or other qualifications which they do not use at work.'

Some qualifications are clearly irrelevant – Theresa May has an Oxford degree (second class) in Geography, which cannot be of much direct use – although a connection with the dreaming spires always helps. Many of those five million, however, are flipping hamburgers, presumably, or riding mopeds with a cargo of pizza (hot from the wood-fired oven). Deliveroo kids, I've discovered, talking fast before my grub cools, are often commendably educated young people. Rain, hail, sleet or snow, the pizza man (BSc Hons) will go. *Buon appetito*.

You have a first-class degree in history? The pound shops need checkout staff on minimum wage. No numeracy required. Machines do the calculations.

The McJob, zero-hours, de-skilled 'gig' jobs offer no benefits: no paid holiday, no sick pay, no employer's pension contribution, no career ladder to professional status employment, no prospect of things ever getting better than minimum payment plus overtime for hard, boring, robotic work. The young, a mass of them worthy of better things, are now living on Planet No. If this isn't a war of attrition against the young, what is it?

What the young were mulcted of was going, via

innumerable invisibly dribbling channels, to the GNP. In short, the young were again paying for the debts run up to shore up the economy after 2008. Austerity doesn't create unemployment. Just the opposite. What it does is create jobs unworthy of those condemned to do them.

Generation Rent

It's an irony that rented accommodation for young people in major conurbations, pre-eminently London, costs as much or more than an average 25-year mortgage would for the same property. The difference is that rent, unlike the average mortgage, creates no lasting asset for the payer – just a month's keeping the wolf from the door. Nonetheless, for many young people today, renting is the only option other than the park bench. The rental industry has been joyously released from the old rent-book and tribunal regime that imposed, as more *dirigiste* governments thought, fairness on the landlord industry.

Nowadays, rentals are a money machine: hence the boom in buy-to-let. Or buy-to-exploit. No more fairness; it's a jungle. Upfront 'deposits' (interest-free loans not always returned), key money, no security of occupation or rights to children, pets and parties. A socially and culturally strangled existence. And expensive with it.

Rents are routinely set at 'what the market can bear'. Students, short-term renters with easy access to the loan tap (to be paid back later), can bear a lot. They raise rent levels for everyone. Including young impecunious marrieds without letters after their name but with young children to care for. It's life blight.

The 'studentification' of whole, previously residential, areas of the London suburbs and other cities raises an occasional furore – students are not, particularly on Saturday nights, the most welcome of neighbours.[16] But, given the exploitative economics, student ghettos have sprung up everywhere there are municipal institutions of higher learning. The old university-run 'student hall' is a thing of the past. Pastoral accommodation is outsourced and up-priced. And very unpastoral.

---

16 See *The Economist*, 1 September 2017, 'Growing Pains'.

In September 2017, the average rent per person or couple in London stood at £1,246 a month, according to the most recent *Countrywide* index. Across the UK it's an estimated average of £927 per person or couple per month. For students, willing to sardine-can it over their three to four years with fellow students, the rental cost was estimated at £780 per month in London, the city with the largest floating student population.[17] Postgraduates, further into their adult years and needing more study space for their research, were advised by the institutions at which they intended to study that total living costs could run as high as £20k p.a.

These wince-making amounts, paid by loan, would become, during the student's lifetime, an interest-accruing debt burden. Three years of fun; forty years paying it off. It does, as said above, douse the fire in the young person's belly. Which, of course, is one reason why it's been allowed to happen. Debt tames, as Orwell said.

Taming is a good thing. Students (2.5 million of them by current count, more than the British army and police

---

17 *Sunday Times*, 24 September 2017.

force combined) are the most disruptive elements in society, because they are the cleverest and have, assetless as they are, least to lose. They must, pro bono publico, be kept down. Expensive hovelising is one way of doing that. Nothing like an unflushing toilet to take your mind off flushing the government.

Camden

NW Camden, where I live, around the 'Lock', is London's *quartier latin*. Ever adaptable, the students and other young people residing in Camden for three or four years put up with squatter-standard accommodation for what the place offers culturally.

Camden Parkway – a short, lively corridor down from Regent's Park to the town's Underground station – used to have a miscellany of shops. When I first came to live in the area, Alan Bennett's Lady in the Van's snake could be imagined slithering out from Palmer's exotic pet shop (monkeys were a speciality) to the Lady of Hal church round the corner in Arlington Road (I must one day find out who the Lady of Hal was).

Bennett himself then lived 500 yards away, opposite Jonathan Miller and other literati and artists in the high-culture enclave of Gloucester Crescent. But Parkway, once a road which symbolised the vibrant heterogeneity of the borough, is now dominated by eighteen estate agents, all principally marketing rented accommodation. The target clientele is, needless to say, the young. They're ideal – they come, they pay, and in a short while they're gone, to make way for the next youthful intake. And they put up with oppressive conditions (such as, for students, paying full rent during vacations).

To sum up. Graduates, even those who find jobs equivalent to their qualifications and ability, will find a less rich (in every sense) life ahead of them. Particularly at the retirement gold-watch stage of life. Young people generally, with degrees or without, are the new deprived. As always, the field of play and its rules have been set by potentates older than them.

A Ladderless World

Noam Chomsky, the Yoda no one (least of all today's

young Luke Skywalkers) listens to, observes that after WWII a hugely indebted US brought in the GI Bill, admitting anyone who had served entrance to higher education, and a vast number of blue-collar benefits (tolerance of trade unionism was primary among them).

It led in the US to the 'Eisenhower Years'. They were appropriately named for a President who, as a Commander in Chief, had won the war for the Allies. It resulted in the 1950s growth of an upwardly mobile, two car-owning, tract house-owning, washing machine-owning middle class. Think *Desperate Housewives*. I remember James Dean, the seventeen-year-old crazy mixed-up kid in *Rebel without a Cause* going to school (school!) in his personal limousine. What did he have to rebel about? The price of gasoline?

America was the envy of the world for many things, but not least for the opportunities it gave its citizens to live well, respect themselves, better themselves and – most importantly – better the prospects of their off-spring. Blue collars became white collars. White collars became Brooks Brothers suits.

As popular series like *Mad Men* suggest, we have

nostalgia for those years – even among those who never experienced them at first hand. Don Draper – working class – by talent and ruthlessness – becomes a power in the world of advertising, the industry that publicised how wonderful the American way of life was.

Which, in fact, after the austerities of war, it was. This was something that had been made to happen. Then, in the 1980s and after, it was made not to happen. It was as if a door slammed shut in the young's face. Higher education, in the best places, now costs $35k p.a., and rising.

During the twenty-five years I spent working in America, I met, in academic life, distinguished colleagues who had ascended from humble backgrounds with the help of the GI Bill. They were now retiring, falling like autumn leaves off the tree. But retiring with a seasonal sense of a fulfilled, not a denied, life. I also met non-academics, can-do guys, who had made themselves multi-millionaires, with the aid of technical higher education supplied by the GI Bill. As Chomsky insists, it shows what could be done by a well-meaning country. It wasn't philanthropy: it was the full use of human resources.

Over Here

The UK was a country on its knees financially and spiritually in 1945. Its population was obliged to feed itself via the ration book (was this what victory meant?) until the early 1950s. I personally recall when sweets 'came off' – the result was there was not so much as a Spangle to be found anywhere in the length and breadth of the country. 'Shortage' was the word of the time.

The country managed nonetheless to bring in the NHS, an open-entry grammar school system and free higher education. And it built homes-for-heroes council house estates. I remember green fields round Colchester, where I lived. A year on, the cows were gone and a housing estate was there – houses with modern facilities like inside lavatories, refrigerators and bathrooms. Those council estates created a stable 'base class' – with life chances beyond the unlikely enrichments from choosing the correct three draws on Littlewoods' football pools. Many of my friends lived in those houses – and some teachers. I did myself (in a 'prefab') for a while. It was better than OK.

Council houses were snapped up when Mrs Thatcher,

thirty years later, decouncilled them and put them on the market, generally beyond the reach of the kind of low-income owners they had originally been created for.

Above all there was, looking back, opportunity for the young in the decades following WWII. Open doors. Or at least ajar doors (only 12 per cent of school leavers could aspire to higher education – until the Robbins expansion of the early 1960s, driven by the principle that university places should be available to 'all who are qualified by ability and attainment to pursue them').

It was partly pay-off. Hundreds of thousands of young men and women, my father among them, had made the 'ultimate sacrifice' (i.e. died, unpleasantly) for their country. Others (including relatives of mine – some of them women) had given up seven of the best years of their life. The country was morally obliged to make some recompense and, to its credit, it did so.

Those who returned could expect a range of social rewards. Good health and nutrition, primarily: children in the baby boom years would go on to grow inches taller than their parents and were spared, by vaccination, from traditional killers.

Trade unions protected workers. For children, like me, education doors were flung open. From a copper-bottomed outside lavatory (toilet paper: cut-up slices of the *Daily Mirror*; best use for the rag, Beaverbrook's *Express* would have said), no fridge, no running hot water, no central heating, no home telephone. From this *echt* working-class background (looked after for some time by council-housed relatives) I received grammar school and higher education which would springboard me, over the decades, into a high-paid (for my background) professional life. Work which did not break my back in my fifties, and which offered great job satisfaction. Fee-free at every stage.

I was not, in the 1960s and '70s, outstanding as regards my abilities. I never fooled myself about that. Nor did I have a winning ticket in life's lottery. No blue blood or family riches. It was the world I was lucky enough to be born in that made me the first Sutherland to reach university.

There were ladders for the young to ascend. And there were no barriers to higher rungs. I retired on the pension whose generous provision no longer exists in my profession.

The various ladders I, and my contemporaries, rose by have been deliberately kicked away. It makes me ache.

Ladderlessness, as I've called it, is the rule of the day. And it is something first willed then tolerated by those who govern our lives. For their ends.

It's not a conspiracy; it's class warfare. Hobbes was right.

David Willetts, a politician who has pondered this issue, wrote to *The Times* the other day (23 September) that the inability to house themselves was distorting young lives of all classes and damaging British society as a whole. We are producing an unanchored generation of drifters.

For many (I'm tempted to say most) young people, getting on the housing ladder is nowadays fraught and more commonly a hopeless dream. Like the one-in-a-million lottery ticket.

Dick Whittington arrived a tramp and died a rich merchant and Lord Mayor of the greatest city in Europe. It may be folklore but it contains a kernel of truth. Dick could aspire. Young people working in a slave plantation-sized Amazon warehouse – only young(ish) people can handle the electronically driven work rate for long – are, most of them, stuck on the ground floor.

They lodge, too many of them, in some form of barrack-room accommodation, or in far-off places requiring hours of (expensive) travel. (Amazon, one should note, is one of the better employers, by today's standards.) However adept they are at handling their daily tasks, the ground-floor Amazonian will never, barring the kind of miracle found in films, get to management level. A key to the executive toilet will never jingle in their pocket.[18]

Disenfranchising the Young

There are any number of reasons why successive administrations have denied the young housing opportunities and what I've called ladders. But to blow off some paranoid steam, there may be an underlying, never stated, reason. The young person's turnout in elections has been, until very recently (with Corbynmania) lamentably low.

---

18 Jeff Bezos, one should note, started his megafirm, as it is now, in a garage.

The commonly advanced reason is that the young think they have more interesting things to do than queue up at a voting station behind some old geezer voting to preserve his £200 Xmas giveaway.

There is, plausibly, another reason, analogous to registration obstacles traditionally placed on African Americans in the US South. The subversive aim is to keep the young out of play. It's typically a hassle for a student to get on the electoral roll. Where do they live? At home (where, perhaps, they first voted at eighteen, and where they know, via their parents, local council affairs)? Or where their university is? If the latter, they are continuously changing address. Sometimes, over the long vacation, they have no address. It can be fixed, but it's a hassle, and even a small hassle creates an impediment. Particularly when exams loom, spring to summer.

Registering students could be made a lot easier. But it isn't. Why? Because when they vote en masse, in a spirit of solidarity, students upset things as they are, as Nick Clegg found to his cost. Sheffield, his former constituency, has many students (enough to cause stu-dentification problems). They combined to eject Clegg for his flagrantly going back, as Deputy Prime Minister, on his 'no fee increase' pledge. The trappings of high office were more important than his word.

Part III

Meet Social Norm

'THERE ARE MORE young adults living with parents than with spouses' was an alarmed headline on front pages in April 2017. It didn't seem right somehow. Against nature. But reliable figures proved it was a fact, in both America and the UK.

The US Census Bureau came up around the same time with the following shocker:

> There are now more young people living with their parents than in any other arrangement … What is more, almost 9 in 10 young people who were living in their parents' home a year ago are still living there today, making it the most stable living arrangement. The Number 1

living arrangement today for Americans in the 18-to-34 age bracket, according to the Census Bureau, is to reside without a spouse in their parents' home.[19]

It was likewise, corresponding surveys revealed, in the UK. It was as if the tides in the ocean had decided to roll in an opposite direction. Leave school then leave home had been the traditional two-step into adulthood. Not come back and cuddle your teddy.

Within living memory, leaving for university (or in my day National Service) severed the second umbilical cord. Many of my working-class friends (whom I found more congenial, in my late, wild drinking teens, than school mates) were married by their mid-twenties. 'Settling down', the phrase was. 'Going under' might have been more appropriate. The fun in their life was over. They got real. And life got harder. Read again the last pages of Sillitoe's *Saturday Night and Sunday Morning* (particularly the last chapter).

As the (old) song went, 'wedding bells are breaking

19 https://www.advisorperspectives.com/commentaries/2017/06/28/
one-third-of-millennials-are-living-with-parents?channel=Income

up that old gang of mine'. Except the gang wasn't old –
just the opposite. And the young marrieds set up their
own nest. Just like the birds do. And you need no orni-
thologist to tell you that if the birds didn't do that they'd
be extinct in a generation.

It was, of course, different for the moneyed, privileged, top tier – the Charles Ryders and Sebastian Flytes
(imagine in your mind's ear the *Brideshead* music). Their
lives ran on class, privilege and cash lubricant.

The image, for the mass of the sub-Bullingdonian
young in those days, was returning the key of the family
door you had received at twenty-one. Then, at around
the same juncture or a bit later, going on to make your
own home.

No longer.

Nowadays, as the American Census Bureau revealed,
one in four US graduates, after they've thrown their
mortar boards in the air, go back, seldom by choice, to
their first family home. Typically the same bedroom.
'Co-residence' is the icy social science term.

For those who never made university, but suffer the
same social pressures, chances are they never left their

81

first home to make a second. They grew too big for the childhood bed – but stayed. One in four young Americans co-residing with parent(s) is a depressing statistic. And it's growing. The most recent figure is 40 per cent.

In the UK, co-residence is reckoned to be a higher figure than the US. Fifty per cent of home recidivism among the nation's young is quoted. Parents tend to dislike this kind of reunion. Bad pennies come to mind. There's a whiff of parental failure. The kid has proved a bad investment. After the prodigal returned, and the fatted calf was killed, did his parents really want the young spendthrift around for ever? Let him go away and fatten his own calves.

A 2017 LSE research survey concluded, in throttled social science speak, 'Living together again is often not a strongly positive experience for parent or child.'[20] Those Paddington posters on the bedroom walls are now melancholy – recalling years when you could dream big.

---

20 http://eprints.lse.ac.uk/61650/1/Lewis_Experience%20co-residence_2016.pdf

The Bank of Mum and Dad may step in (for the few)

Breakfast, in adulthood, with Mum and Dad is not such a good thing. And that awful question over the cornflakes, 'What are you going to do today?'

As it happens, the Bank of Mum and Dad is not as reliable a facility as cosy widespread reference to it implies. According to the insurance firm Wesleyan, parents would need to set aside £163 every month from the day their child is born until they reach twenty-one to cover the £51k cost of a university degree.[21] Should they wait until the child is sixteen to start saving, the cost will be close on a thousand a month. These are, for most, deterrent sums. And when you look at current house prices wholly deterrent.

Some 3.3 million UK adults aged between twenty and thirty-four were living in the parental home in 2013. Slightly more in the following four years, I'd guess. And an awful lot fewer did so thirty years earlier.

These millions amounted to a quarter of their age

---

21 Reported in *The Guardian*, 19 August 2017.

group. But among graduates aged twenty-two to twenty-four, the proportion 'rose to about half', according to the LSE researchers.

The LSE report concluded that with up to half of new graduates living at home, co-residence 'may become a new social norm'. One sees Social Norm skimming the job ads online, fiddling with his CV on the job-search site, then going down the pub to spend what's left of his JSA. He hangs out in the afternoon until it's decent to watch TV in his bedroom and do a bit of social networking. Thirty is not that far distant. But he suppresses that awful thought. Social Norma has a similarly vacuous day – perhaps a bit more chatter and helping out with the housework.

The effect is socially disintegrating. You cannot put an adult life together, living in the bedroom where you listened to bedtime stories and explored the excitements of solitary sex (forgive the grossness) – but are unable to have partnered sex. Your parents wouldn't like it.

The effect of the above back-to-home statistics is to neuter the younger generation. Render them socially harmless. Keep them in baby harness. And it has been allowed to happen for another reason. It removes from the government any need to spend their money on the construction of the houses the young need. That money can go to public funds and buy an aircraft carrier or two.

Knock-Ons

There is a likely relationship between young adult and parental co-residence and another recent phenomenon, the decline of marriage and the nuclear family. On 13 July 2016, the BBC website reported the following 'tipping point', from the ONS, under the headline 'Marriage on the Decline as Singles Rise'. It's worth quoting at length:

> The percentage of people aged 16 and over in England and Wales who are married has fallen to its lowest level since 2002, official figures show. In 2015, 50.6 per cent of the population was married, compared with 54.8 per cent in 2002, the Office of National Statistics says.
>
> The second largest category – single, never civil partnered or married – grew from 29.6 per cent to 34.5 per

cent during this time. 'Cohabitation has become more common as an alternative to marriage, especially at younger ages,' the ONS says.

Although marriage has also declined among the middle-aged. The divorced or widowed made up a smaller proportion of the total population in 2015, at 8.1 per cent and 6.5 per cent respectively, the widowed population falling from 8.1 per cent in 2002, after continuing increases in life expectancy, particularly for men.

The smallest group was the civil partnered, making up 0.2 per cent of the population aged 16 and over in 2015. ONS statistician Pamela Cobb said: 'Just over half of the population aged 16 and over were married in 2015. This figure has steadily declined since 2002, which could be associated with a rise in cohabiting among those who have never married or formed a civil partnership.'

What was the advice that used to be given young people? 'Get a job: keep the job. Get married: stay married.' No more. It's zero-hour work without 'prospects', and 'cohabitation' – or just the regular (if you're lucky) one-night stand or short affair.

To quote another dismal finding by the ONS, marrieds, as a group, are shrinking fast: 'Cohabitation has become more common as an alternative to marriage, especially at younger ages.' Less than half the young population of the UK marries, or expects to marry. Transient relationships are the norm.[22]

There are many reasons: less shaming of promiscuity, better contraception, and legal abortion are three. But another factor is the inhibition of two recent graduates marrying, with a negative joint dowry of £100,000 debt. It takes the icing off the cake.

Second Knock-On

Without families – solemnised or not, gay or straight, extended or nuclear – children's development is less sure. It has been called the child's marriage premium. An exhaustive study by the Institute for Fiscal Studies came up with the following last year:

---

22 https://www.thespruce.com/cohabitation-facts-and-statistics-2302236

- By the time children are aged 3, there are already statistically significant differences in child outcomes between children born to married parents and those born to cohabiting parents. On average, children born to married parents display better social and emotional development and stronger cognitive development than children born to cohabiting parents.

- The differences in children's social and emotional development are much larger than the differences in their cognitive development at both age 3 and age 5.

- The most negative outcomes for children are, on average, amongst those whose biological parents have split up, regardless of the formal marital status of the parents before they split.

A 40 per cent advantage for the children of marrieds was discovered at every subsequent important stage of life. There is no need to dwell on this. The case is proven.

One of the reasons certain figures invariably top the *Sunday Times* rich list is that their families are the tightest, most self-binding, in the land and have been so for generations. Blue blood is a prime example.

The 7 May 2017 *Sunday Times* supplement bore the eye-catching title 'The 15 aristocrats who are richer than the Queen'. HM comes a measly 329th equal in the rich list with a £360 million pittance.

Aristocrats are rich because of (1) primogeniture, which supports a single-family lineage and the transgenerational passage of wealth down that line. (2) Over generations, the money piles up by compound interest. (3) The richer you are, the smarter the lawyers you can afford. (4) The richest families (glance at the *Tatler*) intermarry with people from families likewise rich as themselves, multiplying joint family assets.

It's an exclusive club and membership is, at current rates, a cool billion. No use saving up for it, you need five generations of heavy savers behind you.

In 2017, one of the top very rich persons of title was Hugh Grosvenor, the 7th Duke of Westminster, hailed by the newspaper as Britain's 'youngest billionaire':

Thrust to the fore by his father's death nine months ago, the 26-year-old has never sought the limelight, but the flurry of media interest sparked by news that the

£9 billion bachelor has a steady girlfriend is a taste of
things to come.

He did not earn that vast sum – how could he? His
stated occupation, unsurprisingly, is estate management.
Curating his pile. And that pile came to him virtually
intact via perfectly legal ruses.

The founder of the Westminster line was his name-
sake Hugh Lupus Grosvenor (1825–99). That Hugh's
main interest in life was racehorses, but he inherited
vast tracts of English land which stayed in the family,
accumulating wealth year by year.

Like the three million poorer Britons mentioned
above, Hugh (the 2017 heir) 'co-resided' with his family after leaving the University of Newcastle with an
upper second (I salute him, by the way, for choosing
a provincial university). But it was a different kind of
co-residence from Social Norm's.

Alec Douglas-Home, when PM, got fed up with Harold Wilson taunting him across the dispatch box as 'the
14th Earl of Home'. He rejoined, 'I suppose when you
come to think of it, Mr Wilson is the fourteenth Mr

Wilson.' It was witty, but not quite on the mark. The cumulative wealth and prestige of fourteen generations rose a man higher than just having the same surname on birth certificates.

Families Again

Not everyone who comes from a stable family and who goes on to co-create with a partner another family themselves is going to end up hobnobbing on the *Sunday Times* rich list with Hugh, 7th Duke of Westminster.

And one should beware of over-romanticising the family. Literature warns us not to do that. Any scene from Ibsen or Strindberg will serve. The wit Samuel Butler quipped that those children who had parents needed orphanages the most. Read Freud's *The Psychopathology of Everyday Life* and you might well assume every family is a bubbling stewpot of anxiety, neurosis and psychic misery. But the fact remains. In the here and now a family framework will help your future, from whatever class you originate. It's worth a little neurosis.

I taught for twenty-five years at Caltech in America.

It's the leading scientific-technological institution in the world, as international league tables reckon such things. I was paid to teach humanities there because George Ellery Hale, a founding trustee, believed that to be the best kind of scientist you needed to be cultivated in art, literature, history and philosophy. Hale was right. Not that it matters here.

At commemoration ceremonies (annual graduation), I was routinely struck by the fact that half the chairs on the Caltech large lawn ('Court of Man', it was called) where the ceremony took place were occupied by Asian families. Something under half the undergraduate body was Asian or Asian American. No demographic surprise. It's an ethnic group which is attracted to science and technology and excels in them.

Their families had typically arrived in the US without any great assets. But as a group, they rise. The salient point was that those gifted young scientists seemed universally to have a family, often without higher education, behind them. Their young were family investments which had richly paid off. It was disinterested investment. They did not expect financial payback (leave that to the student financial aid companies). One could feel the familial pride. And admire it.

As a Jewish friend told me, ruefully, it used to be Jews, but two generations in southern California and, as the Jewish proverb has it, the blood runs thin. They go hippy in the sun. My wife's surf instructor, a charming, gifted man, fits this bill exactly.

The fact remains that a solid family, interested in its child's future, is the best starting blocks that child can have. State attempts to abolish the nuclear family – as in the 1920s USSR, or some early kibbutzim in Israel – prove the point by their failure. Margaret Mead's *Coming of Age in Samoa* was a hugely influential tract in the 1960s. It created a sense that the nuclear family could be transcended, via tribalism, into hippy communes. Those that did not mutate into cults generally failed. Woe to the society which, as ours is doing, wilfully destroys the family. If I sound like Melanie Phillips, so be it.

Breakdown of family structure in the UK, whether into single parents or 'blended' post-divorce groupings, is chancier for the very young. This state of affairs, manifestly, has been 'let happen'. Because, to repeat the point, the powers that be are frightened by strong, clever, angry young people when they combine around a common interest inimical to the old.

How it has been made to happen can be shown by a single example. In the US, couples can file their tax jointly and get a useful deduction. In the UK, the 'married couple's allowance' was (temporarily) abolished in 2000. Partly it was because marriage as an institution was melting like an ice cube in a microwave. And partly because long-term relationships outside marriage are hard to define.

But partly also, one must suspect, for more purposive reasons.

The British tax system sets up, as the norm, a society of 'singletons' enjoying a spurious kind of freedom – the freedom, as the French jest has it, to sleep under the Seine bridges at night rather than in the Crillon.

Universal Credit will similarly 'singletonise' its millions of recipients. Atomisation – inhibition of forming affiliation groups – is evident everywhere the young congregate. Dissolve the family into single units and other frameworks melt away. There is no past from which one evolves, no future which one creates. Living for the moment, instant gratification, becomes the rule. Do young people 'save up' (as the term used to be) any more?

Why should they, if they can't clearly see any future ahead of them beyond tomorrow morning? Putting money away used to be a discipline for the young. Somewhere, I can't now lay my hand on it, there is a yellowing booklet of my 'savings stamps' with an angelic Prince Charles on it which my primary school class offered every Monday morning, after prayers. When I was nine, I opened my own GPO savings book. Look after the pennies and the pounds will look after themselves was the motto.

One of the cunning ploys of the older generation has been, by cultural change, to disintegrate the world of the young. To fragmentise them. Make them not force and energy but particles. There was some recent confirmation of this US/UK trend in the *New York Times*. On 3 September 2017, Frank Bruni published an article entitled 'The Real Campus Scourge'. Not fees, he argued, but loneliness. A UCLA professor wrote in describing his first-year students at their first meeting. They were 'each standing alone and staring at their phones'. As the course progressed, there was no networking, no friendships, not even the odd feuds. Just solitary eyes staring at phones, or their owners hurrying away, friendless. There were a number of letters recording similar experiences.

Campus community used to be a mosaic of small groups within a general sense of institutional belonging. Who wears 'university scarves' any more? No reason to: there's no belongingness. It's what the sociologist David Riesman called the Lonely Crowd. Facebook doesn't mend it. You can have a thousand followers on Facebook and still be lonely. The lonely electronic crowd.

There are a number of deducible reasons for the fragmented communities of the young our society has knowingly brought about. Many universities, UCLA among them, are nowadays city sized. You have no more reason to feel connected to the person sitting next to you in the refectory than the person you stand next to in the rush hour underground. You're just peeved that there are so many people next to you. Loneliness, outside Samuel Beckett drama, is an unhealthy condition.

And now, among the young, unhealthily widespread. Unsurprisingly, mental illness in the young is on the rise – despite the profuse sweeteners of life they have.

The Reason for All This

The new programmes that oppress the young are, one has to suspect, designed to disarm and control them. These circumstances, to repeat the point, have not merely happened, they have been let happen and made happen for evident reasons. There is a dominant historical reason. To understand it, return half a century to 1967/68, the 'year of the young rebels', as Stephen Spender (not young at the time) called it. It was the nearest to youth-fired revolution North America and Europe (particularly France) came in the twentieth century. You had to be there to know how it frightened the authorities – call them the old guard, whose defences suddenly seemed vincible. Old men, by the way, do not, *pace* Shakespeare, forget.

The really dangerous element in the late '60s was that the angry young were politicised and idealistic. It wasn't hooligan outrage or a football fan fracas. The young had their philosophers – Marcuse, Althusser, Angela Davis. They had poster heroes (Che and Mao).

Put together large numbers of students of this enlightened kind, with a common cause, and you will have serious risks with social stability – things as they are. In France, students, in alliance with trade unions, came close to bringing about a second revolution. *Les événements*, the authorities called it. 'Events, dear boy', to echo Harold Macmillan's well-known explanation about what made running a country tricky.

The Conservatives are intelligent enough to conserve: their reason for being (not unreasonable) is to keep things as they are. They do it consummately well. Barring a few radicals, the Labour Party, cleaving to the centre, has – until Corbyn – gone along with the same policy.

The authorities saw a number of remedies to the late '60s/early '70s insurrection. One was to admit more women into universities and other high places in society, hitherto unwelcoming. There had been other 'permissive' concessions to youth pressure. The 'Lady Chat' lifting of censorship on literature. The Sexual Offences Act (abolishing the cruel stigma on homosexuality). The legalisation of abortion, giving women the right to choose.

More effective, behind the scenes, was the abolition of higher education's independence – bringing the universities which had spawned such terrifying disorder under state indoctrinal control. Not, at this stage by student fees but, initially, by directive funding, via the University Grants Committee, as it then was.

It used to be, by the old quinquennial system, that the University Grants Commission would come up to the higher education wall and toss a bag of gold over it, with the cheery shout – see you again in five years. Spend as you like but spend well.

Cuts and a freeze of the university finances were the government's first disciplinary measures. Less gold. Put purse string around a person's or institution's throat and they come to their senses. This, bringing the universities to heel by finance, was followed by accountability – were the universities doing a good job? If not, another tug on the purse string.

Inspectorisation – outside judgement of the quality of research (initially RAE) and teaching (initially TQA) – led on to league tables. The results were determined by gladiatorial combat. University vs University. Success, particularly in research, was financially 'consequential'. Institutions of higher education now fought with each other for eminence and the money that went with it. There were changes in top management. CEOs experienced in the real worlds of industry and commerce were hired – typically with huge pay increases. The final phase, with us now, was to hose student brain power into areas of knowledge the state thinks valuable to itself, in a competitive global economy. Science, medicine, economics and engineering, primarily.

Postwar universities were until the late '60s competing on a level playing field. Aberystwyth and Balliol College received equal sacks of gold over their walls. As I write, Oxford and Cambridge have been judged, principally by the quality and quantity of their research, the world's best. Hip hip. The results in funding (via endowment and investment) are visible and will, for a certainty, make the top institutions even more top.

Lower social-scale youth was bought off with sex, drugs and rock 'n' roll: the modern bread and circuses. They could make as much noise as they wanted, so long as it wasn't political noise. Hedonism was presented as liberation. But the effect was unliberatingly narcotic. Access to alcohol was ever less licensed. Possession of drugs 'for personal use' was, in large part, decriminalised. Cheap, stylish designer clothes and easy access to popular, electronically delivered music stimulated a hectic obsession with throwaway fashion and culture. Keeping up with the latest music, via the iPod and iPhone, was virtually a second job. The Saturnalian package holiday to Ibiza and elsewhere offered the ecstasies of orgy. One firm summed up what they offered in the name: 'Carnage'.

How does that song by the Vengaboys go?

I don't wanna be a busdriver

All my life

I'm gonna pack my bags and leave this town

Grab a flight

Fly away on Venga Airways

Fly me high
Ibiza sky

'Let them not eat the sweets which are their poison,' says the wily old politician in Shakespeare's *Coriolanus*. The young, as a conglomerate group, were given, from the mid-'90s, treats and sweets which no other generations of young people have enjoyed. It kept them quiet politically. No more 1968. (Jeremy Corbyn, nineteen years old in that year, surely remembers.)

Education, Education, Education

Traditionally, patriarchy's way of keeping young males down was to send them off to war or conscript them into peacetime armies ('National Service', the 'Draft'). They would learn 'duty' and make themselves less troublesome thereafter.

There is, I can testify, nothing like ten weeks' army basic training for hollowing out a youngster and filling him with subservience ('Attenshun! You 'orrible little man'). Young women? Marriage and childbearing would do for them. In war, they could take up jobs left by fighting men. But when it was over it was *Kinder*, *Kuche und Kirche* for Rosie the Riveter. Feminism has, thank God, changed all that. But not entirely.

The popular idea of war has been warped by movies – John Wayne or Frank Sinatra doing derring-do on celluloid (both men cannily avoided the real thing, 1941– 45). As Kurt Vonnegut (who did not avoid it) tells us in the best novel to come out of WWII, *Slaughterhouse Five*, every war is a Children's Crusade.

A lot of young people died in the Great War (1914–18), many more than in 1939–45. It was a juvenile holocaust inspiring that poem by Wilfred Owen, imminently to be a casualty himself, 'Anthem for Doomed Youth'.

> What passing-bells for these who die as cattle?
> Only the monstrous anger of the guns.
> Only the stuttering rifles' rapid rattle
> Can patter out their hasty orisons.

A German shell silenced his poetry. The telegram announcing his death came with the 'passing bells' announcing amnesty. Field Marshal Haig, whose strategy had directed Owen up the line to death, survived to the ripe old age of sixty-six. Hip hip.

In the twenty-first century, the whole nature of war has evolved from First World War mud, blood and whizz-bangs to something wholly mechanised. Conflict is roboticised, drone driven or rocket propelled. The qwerty keyboard and satellite camera are frontline weapons. Modern armies already have armaments SF couldn't have dreamed of, fifty years ago. They don't need 'Poor Bloody Infantry'. The nearest most nineteen-year-olds will come to 'real' war is their Xbox. The British army is now reduced to 80,000 (the size of a Wembley crowd).

In the 1990s, a clever scheme was hatched from the fertile brain of Tony ('Education, Education, Education') Blair. Warmongering old-style, as a means of youth control, was passé. Anyone could see that. Nor would Blair have thought it right.

What then to do with the young? Blair's solution was simple. Don't send the brightest and best to the square-bashing parade ground. Lock them up in ivory

towers, then make them pay for the ivory. The professo-
riate is middle-aged to aged and it has a sergeant-major
power over curriculum – what you are to learn – and
examination results – how well the professors judge
you've learned. Your degree class may likely determine
the social class you belong to for the rest of your life.
It creates anxiety about 'results'. Anxiety usefully fos-
ters obedience. The second, more necessary, step was
to manacle the young to indissoluble, career-long educational debt. That too induced anxiety and servility.

Now, record-breakingly, the UK sends up to 50 per
cent of the brightest and best of the young to university (at their own expense), with the career prospect, for
many, after they've thrown their mortarboards in the
air, of flipping burgers with fifty thousand (plus interest) in 'educational debts' against their name.

Fifty per cent being admitted to university is too
many. Any honest academic will tell you that (though
the university accountants see no objection). But mass
higher education served the social purpose which had
brought it about. The £9,250 annual UK fees were not
voted for by students. They were imposed by their

elders. And they were not for the students' benefit. Nor will fees make universities, and their products (graduates and research), qualitatively better. Since it's now a competitive market, the universities maximise their paying customer base – take as many qualified applicants, home and foreign (the latter preferable) as they can squeeze in. How do you cram 15,000 students into a university space designed for 8,000? Ask everyone to breathe in.

Numbers explode community, creating the Lonely Crowd effect described above. At the mundane level it means no vacant desk in the library, long queues in the (privatised, for profit) refectory, no one-to-one tutorials (grossly inefficient use of time). You go through three years without any teacher being able to put your name to your face, or an identity to your written assignment. One survey in *The Guardian* discovered that 'even in the elite Russell Group' undergraduates would be lucky to get thirty hours' 'one to one' tuition in three years. Sticker price: fifty grand.

These disempowering facts are recorded time and again in the form of student complaint. Cash nexus changes everything in the ivory tower. It's counter-intellectual. So are the gross numbers of firsts and 2:1s now thrown around like wedding confetti.

What rubs salt into the wound are three irritants:

1. Overseas students pay considerably more, and pay up front. Space is made for them and, necessarily, robbed from home students, who are shouldered out from the elite institutions foreigners pay good money for to decorate their CVs.
2. Many departments could not operate as teaching facilities without postgraduate teachers, paid on a gig basis. Most of them are hoping it is a foot in the door. It isn't.
3. And, of course, there are the inordinate payments for VCs able to fix their own salaries because they sit on the committees that set them. Troughs, oink oink. Those huge salaries are, of course, clipped off from the student fee revenue.

As regards the last, take the following example.

Meet Professor Holmes

Cartoonists of a Gerald Scarfe disposition are in two minds whether to portray the present generation of university vice-chancellors (they're increasingly desirous to call themselves presidents) as trough-hogging pigs or cream-slobbering fat cats.

The University of Bolton appointed Professor George Holmes to lead them in 2008, two years after the institution was promoted from a technology college. Professor Holmes has attracted screaming headlines for his ideas on how modern institutions of higher education should be run. They are radical ideas.

The following, for example, headlined in the *Telegraph* (1 August):

UNIVERSITY CHIEFS SHOULD NOT BE ASHAMED OF THEIR SALARIES, SAYS YACHT-OWNING VICE-CHANCELLOR.

On land, the article went on to reveal, Professor Holmes liked to make a splash at classic car rallies, showing off his own classic vehicles. Professor Holmes enjoys, in

2017, an annual salary of £222,120 (£70,000 more than the PM), plus benefits. A bridging loan of a million for housing is reported.

Insufficient, he complained to the *Financial Times*:

> Those at the top end of the sector are not paid enough.
> Nine Australian VCs earn more than A$1 million a year.
> Thirty university presidents in the US do. At Yale it
> is $1.2 million while Oxford pays £300,000. These are
> mobile jobs. If we cut people's pay they will simply
> go abroad.

The Ivy League, we should understand, are fighting tooth and nail to get at Mr Holmes. 'I have had a very successful career,' he continued. 'I hope students use their education to get a good job and then they can have a Bentley. Do you want to be taught by someone who is successful or a failure?'

Professor Holmes has inspired the most scathing academic Wikipedia entry I've ever read (now, sadly, edited), written, one fantasises, by a former student who has failed to acquire their Bentley. It opens 'George

Holmes was born to a property developer' and records an unimpressive intellectual career. Perhaps it's biased.

Appended to the article is the fact that the University of Bolton does not feature in the *Times* universities league table 'as it does not produce enough research papers'. It is ranked 124th out of 128 universities.

Satire is too easy. High-paid VCs, such as Professor Louise Richardson (£350,000 p.a.) at Oxford can legitimately claim they put their institutions at the head of that league table. But for students it is only too obvious that without their fees these gargantuan pay-offs would not be possible. Footballers are paid more, Richardson blandly observed.

Holmes is crass. But he makes a point – the purpose of universities is now centred on finance not production (of highly qualified graduates and research). Chomsky reminds us that General Electric makes more money nowadays playing the financial markets than producing energy for the American population. Universities have been financialised. The old benefit from that; the young do not.

The Customer Is Always Right

The cost of higher education draws students magnetically towards courses which will prove revenue-rich in later life: law, medicine, accountancy. Humanities – and the enrichment they give – is Mickey Mouse. Not worth the iconic fifty thousand. Lecturers, the phrase was, used to 'give lectures' – now they sell them. There used to be 'tutorials' – etymologically, the word signifies your 'private guardian'. Now it's 'contact hours', and precious few of them.

The corrupting effect of university marketisation is to convert students 'reading' a subject (as the phrase once was) into 'customers' – not buying an education but purchasing a degree. The result? Grade inflation. The customer is always right. You don't believe that, fail them in their final exams and keep the department's lawyer's number handy.

The Loan Pit

While they are at university, in easy street, students are

eligible for loans and inviting come-ons from banks. It's a good time to hook the clients in. Over a lifetime, we're told, people change their spouse more often than their bank.

The come-ons are tempting. *The Guardian* recently ran an article under the quizzical headline 'A Free Railcard or a £2,000 Overdraft?'[23] It went on to list the inducements for incoming students in order of attractiveness. Topping the list was Barclays' three-year free overdraft (with a rolling limit of £1,000). HSBC slyly throws in a £60 Amazon voucher and Santander a four-year 18–25 railcard (30 per cent off every off-peak ticket). All bait on the hook.

Most first year students would by this stage be no stranger to the plastic cash lubricant. NatWest ran a TV ad in summer 2017 showing a young girl, aged (to the eye) around thirteen, reading out a plaintive poem she had written to her mum, asking Mum to trust her with a card. She's up and ready. The ad was, one learned, pushing the NatWest 'child's bank account', for 11–18-year-olds.

---

23 https://www.theguardian.com/money/2017/aug/19/how-pick-best-student-account-giveaways-interest-free-overdraft.

In a more paranoid moment one could think of it like the pusher's free first hit of heroin. The bank giveaways for the undergraduate are the second hit.

The little girl, let's fantasise, is now eighteen: going up to 'uni' as she would call it. She has a generous loan facility, with the flash of the card she is now well used to. Given the loan facilities allowed her as an undergraduate, she can flash it promiscuously.

Switch, now, to a feature in the *Evening Standard* of 16 August 2017 on 'luxury student digs'. The venerable word 'digs' originates in the long-ago view that, as regards accommodation, undergraduates might as well get a shovel and dig themselves a trench (call up any episode of *The Young Ones* on YouTube).

Now, springing up in major urban areas are custom-built five-star student apartments with gyms, spas, concierges, TV and WiFi connection in every room, spacious utility areas with washing machines, and all the luxuries of a hotel.

The cost? Between £1,200 and £1,500 a month with a one-year lease (a penalty if broken). These sums are more than some mortgages being paid round the corner.

THE WAR ON THE YOUNG

There were, in 2017, 76,383 purpose-built 'student bed accommodations' of this luxurious kind in London, and more being put on the market every month. There's gold in them thar students.

John Lewis, to synchronise with the A-level results and application season, in August 2017, published a glistening pull-out catalogue: 'Off to university? We've got it covered', advising, with price tags discreetly attached, how the tyro student might appoint their apartments. It portrayed in glowing imagery such necessary accoutrements as a 'Gingham soft-touch alarm clock' at £39 and a John Lewis ('personalise your space!') pen pot. A snip for only £5. The range goes up to £600 for a PC ('the perfect partner'). Everything purchasable by debit card.

How can a young person, who has never earned a penny in their life so far, afford a John Lewis lifestyle? Many decades older would strain. For the few well off and well inclined without too many siblings, the irritatingly called Bank of Mum and Dad might step in. For most students in higher education it was the bank of plastic. One returns to the Orwellian rule: the more you indebt young people, the more controllable they will be.

'SLC': You Don't Know What that Acronym Means? Eleven Million Students Now Do

The government has passed the responsibility for the recovery of student debt on to the Student Loan Company. It is a facility organically connected with, but not run by, Whitehall. It was reckoned more efficient to have a single-minded department do the dirty work. Collecting repayment via the HMRC is easy enough, by deduction, for those former students who file tax returns and are subject to PAYE. But the self-employed, a growing sector, do not.

At times the SLC has been reduced to desperation. For a while it made use of a fictional debt collection agency and threatening letters of the 'pay up or else' kind. By 2017 the SLC had hiked interest rates to 6.1 per cent at the top end of repayers. The point one digit makes it look like precise calculation, not bag snatching.

The repeated mantra is that not until you earn £21k+ (after 2017, £25k) salary will payment be exacted by the HMRC, and the majority of debtors, over thirty years, won't pay in full. It means, however, that those who stay the course will have to pick up the slack for those who don't. For a certainty the already high interest rate will rise to balance the books. The SLC is not a charity.

Some preliminary facts.

- You can't annihilate the debt by bankruptcy.
- The loans, first introduced at a modest level, leapt from £3k to £9k plus, retroactively applied to those still on their degree course.
- As things now look, predictions are that the fees will be £10k p.a. by 2020.
- Student debt repayment is not tax deductible.

The whole fee system is built on an initial misapprehension. It was originally thought only the top institutions would dare go the whole nine-grand hog. You'd pay the full whack at Oxbridge and considerably less at Scumbag University (another *Young Ones* joke). But virtually every university went max. Call it free enterprise.

One thing, in 2017, payees seem to have agreed on: the SLC is Kafka.

The Guardian has run a regular series of denunciatory

articles. The SLC is perceived to be in meltdown. It manifestly can't seem to hold on to its CEOs, some of whom have departed with a whiff of scandal. At the time of writing, it seems not to have a leader. It's a headless chicken, jerking not moving.

Many clients can't, it's reported, get an up-to-date amount of what they owe. It takes weeks, others complain, to get a written reply to the simplest of questions. There are infuriating hold delays to telephone and, when it comes, an unfriendly response. It was reported in *The Guardian* on 5 August 2017 that it was often difficult to stop the SLC absent-mindedly sucking money from earnings after the loan had been wholly paid off. Those complainants have grown in number year by year: 86,000 is the current figure of those made to overpay.

The most serious allegation is that the SLC isn't doing what it was set up to do: create smooth running financial machinery for the distribution and recovery of funds. The commentator Patrick Collinson, in a ferocious article in *The Guardian* on 19 August 2017, opened with the accusation: 'Let's face it, students are likely the victims of mis-selling.' SLC loans, he alleged, are 'overpriced, badly administered, and probably mis-sold'. The SLC loans belong, Collinson alleges, in any 'worst-buy' column. He contrasted the 6.1 per cent current interest rate with Asda loans of 2.9 per cent. He ventured that SLC could be accused of 'shameless profiteering'. Dealing with them was a 'bureaucratic nightmare'. There were faulty penalty charges, lost paperwork and unjustified delays in recompensing for faulty charges.

As in much else, the UK follows its transatlantic leader. US financial aid (as they prefer to call it), which has been running decades longer, has a debt mountain of $1.4 trillion plus. By 2010, student loan debt exceeded credit card debt. There are an estimated seven million defaulters among the 43 million debtors, and collection, via private agencies, is 'rigorous'. Not to say barely this side of leg-breaking. In the UK, the student loan total is currently £100 billion and rising. And still relatively unrigorous.

Mismanagement is serious. But the importance of debt is that it controls: it is the yoke on your shoulders. Light or heavy, it's a yoke, and identifies you as a beast of burden. In the process, it disarms the cleverest in society.

University Fees a 'Ponzi Scheme'

Does the current government, in its heart of hearts, believe that university fees are a fair deal for students? The above title was a front-page headline in the *Telegraph* on 17 August 2017. It directed the reader to a column inside the paper by Nick Timothy, who had been in the very recent past a kitchen cabinet adviser to Theresa May, along with Fiona Hill. They were regarded by many as Mr and Mrs Rasputin. The pair were, it was even more fancifully alleged, effectively governing England through the PM, their servile Maybot. Both resigned, under the pressure of vengeful publicity, after May fell from grace, in the 'catastrophic' June 2017 general election. Timothy had been particularly vilified by the party because he was credited as the creator of the 'dementia tax'. It was a sensible scheme, but poison in the voting booth.

Timothy's column in the *Telegraph* opened with a vignette of his barber (odd since Timothy's almost as bald as the proverbial coot). The young man with the brush and comb had, it emerged, graduated from Southampton Solent University with a degree in Football Studies.

Timothy's point, trenchantly made, was that the fee structure was pointless. It encouraged young people, like his barber, to pay for higher education which would prove useless to them. It cost virtually as much, in terms of administration and defaulters, as the old grants and it rendered British students the most indebted in the developed world. Worst of all, in Britain and the US, it encouraged institutions to raise fees to the maximum and expand enrolment. The more customers the merrier.

College tuition in the US currently costs between $23,000 and $32,000 per annum. The undergraduate course over there is four years. Tuition rises, year on year, faster than average income levels. And, of course, you can't eat college tuition money for lunch or pay your rent with it. You need supplementary loans on top.

If, in the US, you're doing a follow-on degree (liberal arts followed by law or medicine followed by dentistry) you can be well on the way to making yourself a negative millionaire before you've received your first deducted pay cheque.

Distribution and debt collection of federal and state loans have been privatised in the US. Currently there is a class action being brought against the largest of the debt collection firms, Navient. The *New York Times* of 18 January 2017 summarises its alleged delinquencies:

> Navient, the nation's largest servicer of student loans, has for years misled borrowers and made serious mistakes at nearly every step of the collections process, illegally driving up loan repayment costs for millions of borrowers, according to lawsuits filed on Wednesday by a federal regulator and two state attorneys general.
>
> Navient handles $300 billion in private and federal loans for some 12 million people – touching about one in four student loan borrowers …
>
> Navient does not make the loans, but it holds lucrative contracts to collect payments each month on behalf of banks, government and other lenders …
>
> Total outstanding student loan debt hovers at more than $1.4 trillion. Student loan debt has surpassed credit card and auto loan debt.

America, as in many other things, is a decade ahead.

Half of US state and private universities are now kept

going not by tax money or endowment, but by student fee revenue. We, chances are, shall move in the same direction. Financial calculation dictates it. The British government is already selling off chunks of the student loan book.

The barber cutting what remains of NT's hair, if he clocked he was cropping a member of the governing class, would, perhaps, have been tempted to reach for his open razor. What had happened to the job he dreamed of? But the pressing question is this. Timothy was as close to the PM as her shadow. Did she think that she was in charge of the biggest Ponzi scheme in British history?

The Mailed Fist

Debt is worthless unless you can enforce payment.

Otherwise the debtor simply flouts the demand. Force is the operative word. The late twentieth-century riots and the Northern Ireland insurgency had made the British authorities skilled and strategic in putting down unwelcome unrest. This was made crystal clear in the series of student fees and freeze protests riots at the end of 2010.

The demonstrations were detonated by the Browne Report in October to the government that cuts should be made and fees uncapped. The government accepted the report's main recommendations. It provoked the largest student protest for a decade under the slogan 'Fund Our Future'.

Fifty thousand protesters, mainly students, from all over the country, swelled the event. A march past Westminster and Downing Street was approved.

It was initially lightly policed – which the Met quickly realised was an error. An unruly group of around 200 protesters broke into the Tory HQ at Millbank and vandalised the place. The NUS organisers tried, but failed, to stop them.

In response, the police resorted to kettling – a controversial but provenly successful control technique. It involved breaking the mass of demonstrators into small groups and encircling them, often for hours, punitively maximising discomfort. Complaints were later made in Parliament – by the Greens, principally, since some of the kettled were schoolchildren who felt they needed a funded future as well.

In follow-up demos in London, the repression tactics got tougher. Horses and truncheons to heads were used. There was, for the authorities, one supremely lucky episode on the 9 December demo. A young Cambridge student was pictured swinging on the Cenotaph flagstaff. Whatever moral high ground the students had begun with was lost.

The picture, which went viral, told it all. The students were not merely unpatriotic, they were insulting Britain. They were the enemy within. Stamp them down.

The police had played their game consummately well. They had converted protest into riot – or allowed it to degenerate into violent disorder. Mass protest, a mighty weapon (it was what destroyed the poll tax), was judged no longer effective by the students and former student debt payers of Britain. The only solution was the ballot box, and only one party, Corbyn's, was offering a solution. They flocked there.

Fightback?

If the streets are no longer where the young could win, there are other fronts. Among surveys of the world's super-rich is a young man with no family wealth behind him. Mark Zuckerberg is thirty-three years old and his worth is currently estimated at $71.5 billion. An awesome sum.[24]

Zuckerberg enriched himself as a young computer scientist at Harvard by creating an internet communication site for the young: Facebook.

Originally a dating and meet-up chat facility for students, it now has two million subscribers. There are as many Facebook users, globally, as Muslims. The prime statistic is telling as regards Facebook's clientele: 47 per cent are thirty-four or under. Much of the interchange is chat – although increasingly it is a platform for advertising and merchandising.

There were some interesting uses of the internet which suggested how Facebook might be weaponised. For example: the nearest in recent years London has

---

24 For a highly critical assessment of Zuckerberg, see John Lanchester, 'You Are the Product', *London Review of Books*, 17 August 2017.

come to anarchy was the youth-led rampage in early August through north London. The police were alleged to have unnecessarily shot Mark Duggan because, to use the terminology which had currency, black lives did not matter to the authorities. The riots (no one called them protests after they started) led to arson, looting and destruction.

What frightened the authorities was not the violence. They could handle that by ways which had been refined since the Peasants' Revolt. What was alarming, as a portent, was the riot's organisation – by instant messaging. There was also, as in 1968, a clear political motivation.

The authorities had a new technology of their own – CCTV. Three thousand arrests were made, many of them made not by on-site arrest but by camera identification. It played as a battle of technologies – a forecast of how future urban conflict might be waged. The courts later resorted to the doctrines of Draco. To have stolen a bottle of water from a looted store, witnessed on screen, invited imprisonment.

There were other indications, less violent, of organised youth resistance. Nick Clegg had been the black beast in the 2010 student protest. He had said he would never go along with the new fee rates and then, as Deputy Prime Minister, he went along. Not for a mess of pottage but for a limousine was the sneer. He was duly voted out in 2017 by a newly energised and organised Sheffield student vote. The young were learning to vote tactically.

Most ominous, for the old, was the Corbymania surge, driven by Momentum. Analysis revealed a huge, youthful boost in the June 2017 election:

> Age was one of the most significant factors in the general election. Under-45s came out in force for Labour, while over-54s voted in greater proportions for the Conservatives than in 2015. Young voters favoured Labour, with 60 per cent of those aged 18–24 voting for Jeremy Corbyn's party, while 61 per cent of over-64s voted Conservative. The Ukip vote collapsed across every age group.[25]

---

25 https://www.theguardian.com/politics/datablog/ng-interactive/2017/jun/20/young-voters-class-and-turnout-how-britain-voted-in-2017

Rachel Sylvester, in *The Times* of 26 September 2017, noted that young people had taken over Momentum, with a view to taking over the party, then the country, if all the dominoes fell into place.

So who will win the intergenerational war? In the past it was the old. Always the old. As things now look, the future, and who will be dominant in it, age-wise, is in the balance. My hunch is that – after fierce turmoil – gerontocracy may well give way to something for which (tellingly) we as yet have no word: how about 'juvenocracy'?[26]

---

26 I confess, I take the name from the 1980s heavy metal rock group.

Conclusion

WHERE WILL IT go? Prediction is complicated by biological fluidities. The young are a constantly erupting volcano, its lava cooling as it reaches middle age. The old are not around very long – before making way for the formerly middle-aged.

What we have now is a frictional condition, consciously created (as I've argued) to the advantage of one side: the old.

My guess is it will hot up, into new kinds of insurgency and repression. Asymmetric warfare, as it used to be called. The young and old have very different weapons at their disposal.

At the moment it could be thought we are in a phoney

war hiatus (as in October 1914, or January 1940). In my view, the war will become real very soon. And very ugly. I hope to God I'm wrong.

Postscript

THE PROVOCATIONS SERIES aims to deliver at bullet speed. But between the first keystroke (summer 2017) and the final proofreading (January 2018) things, relevant to *The War on the Young*, have happened. Unexpectedly, it's fair to say.

It began with the toppling of a potentate: 65-year-old Harvey Weinstein. The push was an article in the *New York Times* on 5 October 2017. The article alleged career-long harassment, and worse than harassment, of young women by the most powerful man in Hollywood. The article provoked apologies and denials from Weinstein and threats from his lawyers.

The defensive measures and counter-attack might have worked in earlier times. Not now. A cascade of accusations, hundreds strong, followed. Weinstein went to earth in an undisclosed sex-addiction clinic. That too might have worked once. Not now. He was well beyond rehab or comeback. Not all the king's men could put Weinstein together again.

In Britain, the cultural potentate who was toppled, a couple of weeks after Weinstein, was 58-year-old Kevin Spacey – a man to whom the nation had been, hitherto, grateful for his raising the Old Vic theatre to world-class status over his eleven years in post as artistic director. Preponderantly, women accused Weinstein for what he was alleged to have done when they were young and vulnerable. The men who levelled their accusations against Spacey, likewise.

There followed, almost simultaneously, the massive #MeToo Twitter-storm. Electronic communication had become electronic community, with one outraged voice.

What was striking was the pusillanimity of authorities who claimed never to have had the faintest idea what was going on under their noses. The chief executive of the Old Vic, who had hired Spacey as the theatre's artistic director, pleaded total ignorance of what was alleged to be persistent and flagrant misconduct and sex crime.

On 14 October, the Academy of Motion Picture Arts and Sciences (the body that gave Weinstein's company all its Oscars) bleated forlornly: 'What's at issue here is a deeply troubling problem that has no place in our society.' The Academy was not apparently troubled before October 2017. Or at least not 'deeply' troubled.

There are different issues raised by the moral turbulence of late 2017. As regards women, the victimisation was, in general terms, twofold. When young, they were likely to be physically harassed or abused. When older (but not old), they were discriminated against professionally, in terms of advancement and salary. In both situations, old men were principally indicted. 'Patriarchs' was the word.

I worked for much of my professional life in what is regarded as the best science school in the world, Caltech. One of the things I was routinely told by geologists is that earthquakes cannot be predicted.

What happened in the last months of 2017 was an unpredicted culture-quake. And, in the dust thrown up, one could make out, or so one might think, the young taking arms against the old. The war, so to call it, was being fought on a new and confusing front.

My own hunch is that the detonator to the moral quake that shook the Western world in late 2017 was the crass sexism of the most powerful man in that world, discussed on pp. 20–24 above. A dirty old man, he would have been called in a more prudish age than ours.

We are living, as the Chinese curse has it, in interesting times. I cannot visualise how peace, or at least peaceful coexistence between the young and the old, will be achieved. But I hope I may live to see it. If not, God help us all.